Sometimes he sat mute and unmoving all morning or crawled about the schoolroom floor oblivious to the other children or to his teacher. At times he had violent temper tantrums. No one knew whether he was retarded or had suffered brain damage at birth. His own parents had judged him mentally defective.

But Dibs was none of these. He was a brilliant, lonely child trapped in a prison of fear and rage, a prison from which only he could release himself. And through psychotherapy and love, he did.

His courageous emergence into reality is a celebration of the true miracle of birth. Written from life, from the deepest human longings and loftiest human dreams, his story is for us all. . . .

Also by Virginia M. Axline
Published by Ballantine Books

PLAY THERAPY

DIBS
IN SEARCH OF SELF

Virginia M. Axline

with an introduction by
Leonard Carmichael

BALLANTINE BOOKS • NEW YORK

A Ballantine Book
Published by The Random House Publishing Group

Published in the United States by Ballantine Books, an imprint of The Random House Publishing Group, a division of Random House, Inc., New York, and simultaneously in Canada by Random House of Canada Limited, Toronto.

BALLANTINE and colophon are registered trademarks of Random House, Inc.

ISBN 978-0-345-33925-6

This edition published by arrangement with
Houghton Mifflin Company

Printed in the United States of America

www.ballantinebooks.com

First Ballantine Books Edition: December 1967

OPM 99 98 97 96 95 94 93 92

To the memory of my mother

HELEN GRACE AXLINE

Introduction

THIS IS THE STORY of the emergence of a strong, healthy personality in a previously deeply disturbed child.

When the story starts, Dibs had been in school for almost two years. At first, he would not talk at all. Sometimes he sat mute and unmoving all morning or crawled about the schoolroom floor oblivious to the other children or to his teacher. At times he had violent temper tantrums. Teachers, the school psychologist and the school pediatrician were painfully puzzled by him. Was he mentally retarded? Did he suffer from a deep-seated mental illness? Had his brain been damaged at birth? No one knew.

The book gives an account of what the author well calls "the search for self" on the part of this, at first, pathetically ill little human being. In the end he emerges, as a result of Dr. Axline's subtle and superlatively skillful clinical help, as a brilliant and able person—a true leader.

The author is already famous throughout the psychological world for her contributions to the theory and practice of play therapy with children. Her book, *Play Therapy: The Inner Dynamics of Childhood,* has deservedly won wide acclaim and acceptance.

Dibs is an interesting and exciting book for the general reader. It can be read with pleasure and especial profit by all parents who are interested in the marvels of the mental development of their children. It can also be read advantageously by professional students of childhood and of the nature of normal and abnormal mental life.

The child described in this book is indeed at first most unusual, but students of psychology and psychiatry have long recognized that many new insights into normal and typical mental processes and into healthy mental development can be gained from the study of the different and exaggerated forms of behavior that appear in atypical individuals. It may also be noted that historically modern psychology owes much to the detailed analysis of single cases. In this connection the early work of Freud and of Morton Prince may be mentioned.

There can be no doubt that one of the great problems of our crowded and technological age is the proper understanding of techniques by means of which lasting changes in personality and behavior can be brought about. *Dibs,* as a study in mental organization and behavior change, is important in this context. No one who reads this book with understanding can ever again think that human psychological growth, success in a schoolroom, or the acquisition of a complex skill can be achieved merely by overt repetition or by the reinforcement of simple patterns of response.

Another new idea emphasized in this book is that the truly deep and effective healing of a disturbed child may help in a very real way the mental hygiene of the child's parents. This is a novel reversal of the old truism that the successful clinical treatment of a child's parents is often the best form of therapy for a disturbed child.

But above all, *Dibs* is good reading! For me it is as exciting as a first-class detective story!

LEONARD CARMICHAEL
Washington, D.C.

Prologue

This is the story of a child in search of self through the process of psychotherapy. It was created out of the experience of a living person—a little boy named Dibs. As this child came forth to meet the abrupt forces of life, there grew within him a new awareness of a selfhood, and a breathless discovery that he had within himself a stature and wisdom that expanded and contracted even as do the shadows that are influenced by the sun and clouds.

Dibs experienced profoundly the complex process of growing up, of reaching out for the precious gifts of life, of drenching himself in the sunshine of his hopes and in the rain of his sorrows. Slowly, tentatively, he discovered that the security of his world was not wholly outside himself, but that the stabilizing center he searched for with such intensity was deep down inside that self.

Because Dibs speaks in a language that challenges the complacency of so many of us, and because he yearns to achieve a selfhood that can proudly acknowledge his name and place in the world, his story becomes everybody's story. Through his experiences in the playroom, at home, and at school, his personality gradually unfolds and enhances, in some gentle way, the lives of others who were privileged to know him.

DIBS IN SEARCH OF SELF

Chapter One

IT WAS LUNCH TIME, going-home time, and the children were milling around in their usual noisy, dawdling way getting into their coats and hats. But not Dibs. He had backed into a corner of the room and crouched there, head down, arms folded tightly across his chest, ignoring the fact that it was time to go home. The teachers waited. He always behaved this way when it was time to go home. Miss Jane and Hedda gave a helping hand to the other children when it was needed. They watched Dibs surreptitiously.

The other children left the school when their mothers called for them. When the teachers were alone with Dibs they exchanged glances and looked at Dibs huddled against the wall. "Your turn," Miss Jane said and walked quietly out of the room.

"Come on, Dibs. It's time to go home now. It's time for lunch." Hedda spoke patiently. Dibs did not move. His resistance was tense and unwavering. "I'll help you with your coat," Hedda said, approaching him slowly, taking his coat to him. He did not look up. He pressed back against the wall, his head buried in his arms.

"Please, Dibs. Your mother will be here soon." She always came late, probably hoping the battle of hat and coat would be over by the time she arrived and that Dibs would go with her quietly.

Hedda was close to Dibs now. She reached down and patted his shoulder. "Come, Dibs," she said, gently. "You know it's time to go."

Like a small fury Dibs was at her, his small fists

striking out at her, scratching, trying to bite, screaming. "No go home! No go home! No go home!" It was the same cry every day.

"I know," Hedda said. "But you have to go home for lunch. You want to be big and strong, don't you?"

Suddenly Dibs went limp. He stopped fighting Hedda. He let her push his arms into his coat sleeves and button his coat.

"You'll come back tomorrow," Hedda said.

When his mother called for him, Dibs went with her, his expression blank, his face tear-stained.

Sometimes the battle lasted longer and was not over when his mother arrived. When that happened, his mother would send the chauffeur in to get Dibs. The man was very tall and strong. He would walk in, scoop Dibs up in his arms, and carry him out to the car without a word to anyone. Sometimes Dibs screamed all the way out to the car and beat his fists against the driver. Other times, he would suddenly become silent—limp and defeated. The man never spoke to Dibs. It seemed not to matter to him whether Dibs fought and screamed or was suddenly passive and quiet.

Dibs had been in this private school for almost two years. The teachers had tried their best to establish a relationship with him, to get a response from him. But it had been touch and go. Dibs seemed determined to keep all people at bay. At least, that's what Hedda thought. He had made some progress in the school. When he started school, he did not talk and he never ventured off his chair. He sat there mute and unmoving all morning. After many weeks he began to leave his chair and to crawl around the room, seeming to look at some of the things about him. When anyone approached him, he would huddle up in a ball on the floor and not move. He never looked directly into anyone's eyes. He never answered when anyone spoke to him.

Dibs' attendance record was perfect. Every day his mother brought him to school in the car. Either she led him in, grim and silent, or the chauffeur carried him in and put him down just inside the door. He never screamed or cried on his way into the school. Left just inside the door, Dibs would stand there, whimpering, waiting until someone came to him and led him into his classroom. When he wore a coat he made no move to take it off. One of the teachers would greet him, take off his coat, and then he was on his own. The other children would soon be busily occupied with some group activity or an individual task. Dibs spent his time crawling around the edge of the room, hiding under tables, or in back of the piano, looking at books by the hour.

There was something about Dibs' behavior that defied the teachers to categorize him, glibly and routinely, and send him on his way. His behavior was so uneven. At one time, he seemed to be extremely retarded mentally. Another time he would quickly and quietly do something that indicated he might even have superior intelligence. If he thought anyone was watching him, he quickly withdrew into his shell. Most of the time he crawled around the edge of the room, lurking under tables, rocking back and forth, chewing on the side of his hand, sucking his thumb, lying prone and rigid on the floor when any of the teachers or children tried to involve him in some activity. He was a lone child in what must have seemed to him to be a cold, unfriendly world.

He had temper tantrums sometimes when it was time to go home, or when someone tried to force him to do something he did not want to do. The teachers had long ago decided that they would always invite him to join the group, but never try to force him to do anything unless it was absolutely necessary. They offered him books, toys, puzzles, all kinds of materials that might interest him. He would never take anything directly from anyone. If the object was placed on a table or on the floor near him, later he would pick it up and examine it carefully. He never failed to accept a book. He pored over the printed pages "as though he could read," as Hedda so often said.

Sometimes a teacher would sit near him and read a story or talk about something while Dibs lay face down on the floor, never moving away—but never looking up or showing any overt interest. Miss Jane had often spent time with Dibs in this way. She talked about many things as she held the materials in her hand, demonstrating what she was explaining. Once her subject was magnets and the principles of magnetic attraction. Another time it was an interesting rock she held. She talked about anything she hoped might spark an interest. She said she often felt like a fool—as though she were sitting there talking to herself, but something about his prone position gave her the impression that he was listening. Besides, she often asked, what did she have to lose?

The teachers were completely baffled by Dibs. The school psychologist had observed him and tried several times to test him, but Dibs was not ready to be tested. The school pediatrician had looked in on him several times and later threw up his hands in despair. Dibs was wary of the white-coated physician and would not let him come near. He would back up against the wall and put his hands up "ready to scratch," ready to fight if anyone came too close.

"He's a strange one," the pediatrician had said. "Who knows? Mentally retarded? Psychotic? Brain-damaged? Who can get close enough to find out what makes him tick?"

This was not a school for mentally retarded or emotionally disturbed children. It was a very exclusive private school for children aged three to seven, in a beautiful old mansion on the upper East Side. It had a tradition that appealed to parents of very bright, sociable children.

Dibs' mother had prevailed upon the headmistress to accept him. She had used influence through the board of trustees to have him admitted. Dibs' great-aunt contributed generously to the support of the school. Because of these pressures he had been admitted to the nursery school group.

The teachers had suggested several times that Dibs needed professional help. His mother's response had been repetitive: "Give him more time!"

Almost two years had gone by and even though he had made some progress, the teachers felt that it was not enough. They thought it was unfair to Dibs to let the situation drag on and on. They could only hope that he might come out of his shell. When they discussed Dibs— and not a day went by that they did not—they always ended up just as baffled and challenged by the child. After all, he was only five years old. Could he really be aware of everything around him and keep everything locked inside? He seemed to read the books he pored over. This, they told themselves, was ridiculous. How could a child read if he could not express himself verbally? Could such a complex child be mentally retarded? His behavior did not seem to be that of a mentally retarded child. Was he living in a world of his own creation? Was he autistic? Was he out of contact with reality? More often it seemed that his world was a bruising reality—a torment of unhappiness.

Dibs' father was a well-known scientist—brilliant, everyone said, but no one at the school had ever met him. Dibs had a younger sister. Her mother claimed that Dorothy was "very bright" and a "perfect child." She did not attend this school. Hedda had met Dorothy once with her mother in Central Park. Dibs was not with them. Hedda told the other teachers that she thought "perfect Dorothy" was "a spoiled brat." Hedda was sympathetically interested in Dibs and admitted she was prejudiced in her evaluation of Dorothy. She had faith in Dibs and believed that someday, somehow, Dibs would come out of his prison of fear and anger.

The staff had finally decided that something must be done about Dibs. Some of the other parents were complaining about his presence in the school—especially after he had scratched or bitten some other child.

It was at this point that I was invited to attend a case conference devoted to Dibs' problems. I am a clinical psychologist, and I have specialized in working with children and parents. I first heard about Dibs at this conference, and what I have written here was related by the teachers, the school psychologist, and the pediatrician. They asked me if I would see Dibs and his mother and then give the staff my opinion before they decided to dismiss him from school and write him off as one of their failures.

The meeting was held in the school. I listened with interest to all the remarks. I was impressed by the impact of Dibs' personality on these people. They felt frustrated and continually challenged by his uneven behavior. He was consistent only in his antagonistic, hostile rejection of all who would come too close to him. His obvious unhappiness troubled these sensitive people who felt its desolate chill.

"I had a conference with his mother last week," Miss Jane said to me. "I told her that in all probability we might have to drop him from school because we feel we have done all we can to help him and our best is not enough. She was very upset. But she is such a difficult person to figure out. She agreed to let us call in a consultant and try one more time to evaluate him. I told her about you. She agreed to have a talk with you about Dibs, and to let you observe him here. Then she said if we couldn't keep him here she would like us to give her the name of a private boarding school for mentally retarded children. She said that she and her husband have accepted the fact that he is probably mentally retarded or brain-damaged."

This remark brought forth an explosion from Hedda. "She'd rather believe he is mentally retarded than admit that maybe he is emotionally disturbed and maybe she is responsible for it!" she exclaimed.

"We don't seem to be able to be very objective about him," Miss Jane said. "I think that's why we have kept him as long as we have and made so much of the little progress he *has* made. We couldn't bear to turn him away and not have some hand in defending him. We've never been able to discuss Dibs without getting involved in emotional reactions of our own about him and the attitudes of his parents. And we're not even sure that our attitudes about his parents are justified."

"I'm convinced he's on the verge of coming through," Hedda said. "I don't think he can bear to keep his defenses up much longer."

There was obviously something about this child that captivated their interests and feelings. I could feel their compassion for this child. I could feel the impact of his personality. I could sense the overwhelming awareness of our limitations to understand in clear, concise, immutable terms the complexities of a personality. I could appreciate the respect for this child that permeated the conference.

It was decided that I would see Dibs for a series of play therapy sessions—if his parents agreed to the idea. We had no way of knowing what this might add to Dibs' story.

Chapter Two

OUT AGAIN INTO THE night where the dulled light obscures the decisive lines of reality and casts over the immediate world a kindly vagueness. Now, it is not a matter of all black and white. It is not a matter of "this is it" because there is no glaring light of unequivocal evidence in which one sees a thing *as it is* and one *knows the answers*. The darkened sky gives growing room for softened judgments, for suspended indictments, for emotional hospitality. What *is,* seen in such light, seems to have so many possibilities that definitiveness becomes ambiguous. Here the benefit of a doubt can flourish and survive long enough to force considerations of the scope and limitations of human evaluation. For when horizons grow or diminish within a person the distances are not measurable by other people. Understanding grows from personal experience that enables a person to see and feel in ways so varied and so full of changeable meanings that one's self-awareness is the determining factor. Here one can admit more readily that the substances of a shadowy world are projected out of our personal thoughts, attitudes, emotions, needs. Perhaps it is easier to understand that even though we do not have the wisdom to enumerate the reasons for the behavior of another person, we can grant that every individual *does* have his private world of meaning, conceived out of the integrity and dignity of his personality.

I took away with me from that meeting a feeling of shared respect and an eagerness to meet Dibs. I had caught the contagious element of impatience with smug complacency that will abandon all hope without trying

once more—always, just once more—to unlock the door
of our present inadequate answers to such problems. We
do not know the answers to the problems interlacing the
field of mental health. We know that many of our impres-
sions are fragile. We realize the value of objectivity and
calm, ordered study. We know that research is a fascinat-
ing combination of hunches, speculation, subjectivity,
imagination, hopes, and dreams, blended precisely with
objectively gathered facts tied down to the reality of a
mathematical science. One without the other is incom-
plete. Together, they inch along the road in search of
truth, wherever it may be found.

So I would soon meet Dibs. I would go to the school
and observe him in the group with the other children. I
would try to see him alone for a while. Then I would visit
his home for a conference with his mother. We would
decide upon a time for the other appointments in the
playroom at the Child Guidance Center. We would take it
from there.

We were seeking a solution to a problem and we all
knew that this additional experience would be only a
small glimpse into the private life of this child. We did not
know what it might mean to Dibs. It was one more chance
to try to catch hold of a thread that might unravel some
bits of insight that could add to our understanding.

As I went down the East River Drive, I thought of
many children I had known—children who were unhappy, each frustrated in the attempt to achieve a selfhood he
could claim with dignity—children not understood, but
striving again and again to become persons in their own
right. Out of projected feelings, thoughts, fantasies,
dreams, and hopes, new horizons grew in each child. I
had known children who had been overcome by their
fears and anxieties, striking out in self-defense against a
world that for many reasons was unbearable to them.
Some had emerged with renewed strength and capacity to
cope with their worlds more constructively. Some had not
been able to withstand the impact of their outrageous
fortunes. And there is no pat explanation; to say that the

child was rejected and not accepted means nothing in understanding the inner world of the child. Too often those terms are only convenient labels tied on as alibis to excuse our ignorance. We must avoid clichés, quick, ready-made interpretations and explanations. If we want to get closer to the truth we must look deeper into the reasons for our behavior.

I will go to the school tomorrow morning, I decided. I'll telephone Dibs' mother and arrange to have a conference with her at their home as soon as possible. I'll see Dibs next Thursday in the play therapy room at the Child Guidance Center. And where will it all end? If he doesn't manage to break through that wall he has built so sturdily around himself—and it is quite possible that he won't—I'll have to think of some other kind of referral. Sometimes one thing works out very well with one child, but not at all with another child. We don't give up easily. We don't write off a case as "hopeless" without trying just one more thing. Some people think this is very bad—to keep hope alive when there is no basis for hope. But we are not looking for a miracle. We are seeking understanding, believing that understanding will lead us to the threshold of more effective ways of helping the person to develop and utilize his capacities more constructively. The inquiry goes on and on and we will continue to seek a way out of the wilderness of our ignorance.

The next morning I arrived at the school before the children came. The rooms occupied by the kindergarten were bright and cheerful, with appropriate, attractive equipment.

"The children will be here soon," Miss Jane said. "I shall be very interested in your opinion of Dibs. I hope he can be helped. That child worries me to death. You know, when a child is really mentally retarded there's an overall consistent pattern of behavior that shows up in his interests and actions. But Dibs? We never know what kind of mood he'll be in, except that we *do* know there won't be any smiles. None of us has ever seen him smile. Or look even remotely happy. That's one reason we've felt that his problem goes far beyond just mental retardation. He is too emotional. Here come some of the children, now."

The children began to arrive. Most of them came in with looks of happy expectancy on their faces. They certainly seemed relaxed and comfortable in this school. They called out cheery greetings to one another and to the teachers. Some of them spoke to me, asked my name, asked why I was there. They took off their hats and coats and hung them up in their lockers. The first period was a free choice period. The children sought out the toys and activities in which they were interested and played and talked together in a very spontaneous way.

Then Dibs arrived. His mother led him into the room. I had only a quick glimpse of her because she spoke briefly to Miss Jane, said goodbye, and left Dibs. He was wearing a grey tweed coat and a cap. He stood where she left him. Miss Jane spoke to him, asked him if he would like to hang up his coat and hat. He did not answer.

He was large for his age. His face was very pale. When Miss Jane took off his cap I noticed he had black, curly hair. His arms hung limply at his sides. Miss Jane helped him off with his coat. He seemed to be uncooperative. She hung up his hat and coat in his locker.

As she came up to me she said quietly, "Well, there is Dibs. He would never take off his coat and hat by himself, so now we do it routinely. Sometimes we try to get him to join one of the other children in some activity—or give him something specific to do. But he rejects all our offers. This morning we'll just let him alone and you can see for yourself what he will do. He may stand there for a long, long time. Or he may start to move from one thing to another. Sometimes, he flits from one thing to another as though he had no attention span at all. Then, again, he'll focus on something for an hour. It all depends on how he feels."

Miss Jane went over to some of the other children. I observed Dibs, trying not to seem to be focusing my attention upon him.

He stood there. Then he turned, very slowly and deliberately. He raised his hands in an almost futile gesture of despair, then dropped them down to his sides. He turned again. Now I was in his range of vision—if he cared to look at me. He sighed, bit his lip, stood there.

One little boy ran up to Dibs. "Hi, Dibs!" he said. "Come play!"

Dibs struck out at the boy. He would have scratched him but the little boy jumped back quickly.

"Cat! Cat! Cat!" teased the boy.

Miss Jane came over and told the boy to go to the other part of the room and play.

Dibs moved over to the wall, near a small table on which were some stones, shells, pieces of coal, and other minerals. Dibs stood beside the table. Slowly, he picked up first one object and then another. He ran his fingers around them, touched his cheek with them, smelled them, tasted them. Then he replaced them carefully. He glanced in my direction. It was a fleeting look toward me, then quickly away. He got down, crawled under the table and sat there, almost completely out of sight.

Then I noticed the other children were bringing their chairs up in a small circle around one of the teachers. It was time for the children to show the others what they had brought to school and to tell some bit of news that was important to them. The teacher told them a story. They sang a few songs.

Dibs, under the table, was not too far away. From his vantage point he could hear what they were saying and see what they were showing—if he wanted to. Had he anticipated this activity of the group when he crawled under the table? It was difficult to say. He stayed under the table until the morning circle broke up and the children went to other activities. Then he, too, moved on to something else.

He crawled around the room, staying close to the wall, stopping to examine many things he came upon. When he came to the wide windowsill where the terrarium and aquarium were, he climbed up beside them and gazed steadily into the big, square, glass containers. Occasionally, he would reach in and touch something in the terrari-

um. Then, his touch seemed deft and light. He stayed
there for half an hour, seemingly absorbed in his observation. Then he crawled on, completing his trip around the
room. Some things he touched, quickly and carefully, then
passed on to something else.

When he came to the book corner, he fingered the
books on the table, selected one, took a chair, dragged it
across the room to a corner, and sat down on it, facing the
wall. He opened the book at the beginning and slowly
examined every page, turning the leaves carefully. Was he
reading? Was he even looking at the pictures? One of the
teachers went over to him.

"Oh, I see," she said. "You're looking at the bird book.
Do you want to tell me about it, Dibs?" she inquired in a
gentle, kindly voice.

Dibs hurled the book away from him. He threw himself
down on the floor and lay stiff and rigid, face down,
immobilized.

"I'm sorry," the teacher said. "I didn't mean to bother
you, Dibs." She picked up the book, put it back on the
table, walked over to me. "Now that was typical," she
said. "We've learned not to bother him. But I wanted you
to see."

Dibs, in his prone position, had turned his head so that
he could watch the teacher. We pretended not to be
observing him. Finally, he got up and walked slowly
around the edge of the room. He touched the paints,
crayons, clay, nails, hammer, wood, drum, cymbals. He
picked them up and put them down again. The other
children went about their business without too much concern for Dibs. He avoided any physical contact with them,
and they let him alone.

Then, it was time to go out and play. One of the
teachers told me, "Maybe he will. Maybe he won't. I
wouldn't bet a nickel either way." She announced that it
was time to go out and play. She asked Dibs if he wanted
to go out.

He said, "No go out," in a flat, heavy tone.

I said I thought that I would go out, it was such a nice day. I put on my coat.

Suddenly Dibs said, "Dibs go out!" The teacher put his coat on for him. He walked clumsily out into the play yard. His coordination was very poor. It was as though he was all tied up in knots, physically as well as emotionally.

The other children played in the sandbox, on the swings, on the jungle gym, on the bicycles. They played ball, catch, hide and seek. They ran, skipped, climbed, jumped. But not Dibs. He walked off to a remote corner, picked up a little stick, squatted down and scratched it back and forth in the dirt. Back and forth. Back and forth. Making little grooves in the dirt. Not looking at anyone. Staring down at the stick and the ground. Hunched over this lonely activity. Silent. Withdrawn. Remote.

We decided that when the children came back into the room and after their rest period, I would take Dibs down to the playroom at the end of the hall. If he would go with me.

When the teacher rang the bell the children all came in. Even Dibs. Miss Jane helped him off with his coat. He handed her his cap this time. The teacher put a record of soft, relaxing music on the phonograph. Each child got out his mat, stretched out on the floor for the rest period. Dibs got out his mat and unrolled it. He put his mat under the library table, a distance away from the other children. He lay face down on his mat, put his thumb in his mouth, rested with the other children. What was he thinking about in his lonely little world? What were his feelings? Why did he behave in this manner? What had happened to the child to cause this kind of withdrawal from people? Could we manage to get through to him?

After rest period the children put away their mats. Dibs rolled his mat up and put it away in the correct space on the shelf. The children were dividing into smaller groups. One group would have a work period and build things out of lumber. Another group would paint or play with clay.

Dibs stood by the door. I went over and asked him if

he would come down the hall to the little playroom with me for a while. I held out my hand to him. He hesitated for a moment, then took my hand without a word and walked to the playroom with me. As we passed the doors of some of the other rooms he muttered something I could not understand. I did not ask him to repeat what he had said. I remarked that the playroom was at the end of the hall. I was interested in this initial response from him. He had left the room with a stranger without a backward look. But as he held my hand I noticed the hard grip. He was tense. But, surprisingly enough, willing to go.

At the end of the hall, under the back stairs, there was a small room designated as the play therapy room. It was not attractive—there was a cold drabness about its lack of color or decoration. It had a narrow window that let some sunlight filter in, but the total effect was gloomy, even though the lights were turned on. The walls were a dingy, buff color with uneven smears of washed spots here and there. Some of the spots were ringed with stains of the paint that clung to the rough surface of the plaster. The floor was covered with dull brown linoleum that was streaked by a quickly swung, not too clean mop. There was a pungent smell of moist clay, wet sand, and stale watercolor paints.

Toys were on the table, on the floor, and on some shelves around the room. There was a doll house on the floor. Each room in the doll house was furnished sparingly with sturdy block furniture. A family of small dolls lay on the floor in front of the doll house. They were heaped there—mother, father, boy, girl, and baby dolls, with an open box containing other miniature dolls nearby. There were a few rubber animals—a horse, a lion, a dog, a cat, an elephant, a rabbit. There were some toy cars and airplanes. A box of building blocks was on the floor. In the sandbox were some pans, spoons, a few tin dishes. There was a jar of clay on the table, some paints and drawing paper on the easel. A nursing bottle filled with water was on the shelf. A large rag doll sat on a chair. In the corner stood a tall, inflated rubber figure weighted on the bottom so that it would resume an upright position after being knocked over. The toys were sturdily made, but they looked worn and roughly used.

There was nothing about the room or the materials in it that would tend to restrain the activities of a child. Nothing seemed to be either too fragile or too good to touch or knock about. The room provided space and some materials that might lend themselves to the emergence of the personalities of the children who might spend some time there. The ingredients of experience would make the room uniquely different for each child. Here a child might search the silence for old sounds, shout out his discoveries of a self momentarily captured, and so escape from the prison of his uncertainties, anxieties, and fears. He brings into this room the impact of all the shapes and sounds and colors and movements, and rebuilds his world, reduced to a size he can handle.

As we entered the room I said, "We'll spend an hour together here in the playroom. You can see the toys and the materials we have. You decide what you would like to do."

I sat down on a little chair just inside the door. Dibs stood in the middle of the room, his back toward me, twisting his hands together. I waited. We had an hour to spend in this room. There was no urgency to get anything done. To play or not to play. To talk, or to be silent. In here, it would make no difference. The room was very small. No matter where he went in here, he couldn't get too far away. There was a table under which he could crawl, if he felt like hiding. There was a little chair beside the table if he felt like sitting down. There were the toys to play with, if he so desired.

But Dibs just stood in the middle of the room. He sighed. Then he slowly turned and walked haltingly across the room, then around the walls. He went from one toy to another, tentatively touching them. He did not look directly at me. Occasionally he would glance in my direction but would quickly avert his eyes if our glances met. It was a tedious trip around the room. His step was heavy. There seemed to be no laughter or happiness in this child. Life, for him, was a grim business.

He walked over to the doll house, ran his hand along the roof, knelt down beside it, and peered inside at the furniture. Slowly, one by one, he picked up each piece of furniture. As he did, he muttered the name of the objects with a questioning, halting inflection. His voice was flat and low.

"Bed? Chair? Table?" he said. "Crib? Dresser? Radio? Bathtub? Toilet?" Every item in the doll house he picked up, named, carefully replaced. He turned to the pile of dolls, and sorted slowly through them. He selected a man, a woman, a boy, a girl, a baby. It was as though he tentatively identified them as he said, "Mamma? Papa? Sister? Baby?" Then he sorted out the little animals. "Dog? Cat? Rabbit?" He sighed deeply and repeatedly. It seemed to be a very difficult and painful task he had set himself.

Each time he named an object I made an attempt to communicate my recognition of his spoken word. I would say, "Yes. That is a bed," or, "I think it is a dresser," or "It does look like a rabbit." I tried to keep my response brief, in line with what he said, and with enough variation to avoid monotony. When he picked up the father doll and said. "Papa?" I replied, "It could be papa." And that is the way our conversation went with every item that he picked up and named. I thought that this was his way to begin verbal communication. Naming the objects seemed a safe enough beginning.

Then he sat down on the floor facing the doll house. He stared at it in silence for a long time. I didn't prod him on. If he wanted to sit there in silence, then we would have silence. There must have been some reason for what he was doing. I wanted him to take the initiative in building up this relationship. Too often, this is done for a child by some eager adult.

He clasped his hands tightly together against his chest and said over and over again, "No lock doors. No lock doors. No lock doors." His voice took on a note of desperate urgency. "Dibs no like locked doors," he said. There was a sob in his voice.

I said to him, "You don't like the doors to be locked."

Dibs seemed to crumple. His voice became a husky whisper. "Dibs no like closed doors. No like closed and locked doors. Dibs no like walls around him."

Obviously, he had had some unhappy experiences with closed and locked doors. I recognized the feelings he expressed. Then he began to take the dolls out of the house where he had placed them. He took out the mother and father dolls. "Go store! Go store!" he said. "Go away to the store. Go away!"

"Oh, is mother going to go away to the store?" I commented. "And papa, too? And sister?" He quickly moved them out and away from the house.

Then he discovered that the walls of the rooms in the doll house could be removed. He took each wall out, saying as he did, "No like walls. Dibs no like walls. Take away all walls, Dibs!" And in this playroom Dibs took away a little of the walls he had built around himself.

In this manner he slowly, almost painfully played. When the hour was up I told him that the play time here was almost over and we would go back to his classroom.

"There are five more minutes," I said. "Then we will have to go."

He sat on the floor in front of the doll house. He neither moved nor spoke. Neither did I. When the five minutes were up, we would go back to his room.

I didn't ask him if he wanted to go. There was no real choice for him to make. I didn't ask him if he would like to come back again. He might not want to commit himself. Besides, that decision was not up to him to make. I didn't say that I would see him next week, because I had not yet completed the plans with his mother. This child had been hurt enough without my introducing promises that might not materialize. I didn't ask him if he had had a good time. Why should he be pinned down to an evaluation of the experience he had just had? If a child's play is his natural way of expressing himself, why should we cast it in a rigid mold of a stereotyped response? A child is only confused by questions that have been answered by someone else before he is asked.

When the five minutes had passed, I rose and said, "It is time to go now, Dibs." He slowly stood up, took my hand, and we left the room and started down the hall. When we were halfway down the hall and the door of his classroom was in view, I asked him if he thought he could go the rest of the way to his room alone.

"That's right," he said. He dropped my hand and walked down the hall to the door of his room by himself.

I did this because I hoped Dibs would gradually become more and more self-sufficient and responsible. I wanted to communicate to him my confidence in his ability to measure up to my expectations. I believed he could do it. If he had faltered, shown signs of it being too much for him to do this first day, I would have gone a little farther down the hall with him. I would have gone all the way to the door of his room with him, if he had seemed to need that much support. But he went by himself. I said, "Goodbye, Dibs!"

He said, "That's right!" His voice had a soft, gentle quality. He walked down the hall, opened the door of his room, then looked back. I waved. The expression on his face was interesting. He looked surprised—almost pleased. He walked into his room and closed the door firmly behind him. It was the first time Dibs had ever gone any place alone.

One of my objectives in building up this relationship with Dibs was to help him achieve emotional independence. I did not want to complicate his problem by building up a supportive relationship, to make him so dependent upon me that it would postpone the more complete development of his feelings of inner security. If Dibs was an emotionally deprived child—and indications were that he was—to attempt to develop an emotional attachment at this point might seem to be satisfying a deep need of the child, but it would create a problem that must of necessity ultimately be resolved by him.

As I left that first play session with Dibs I could understand why the teachers and the other staff members could not write him off the books as a hopeless failure. I had respect for his inner strength and capacity. He was a child of great courage.

Chapter Three

I TELEPHONED DIB'S MOTHER and requested a conference with her as soon as we might arrange one. She said that she had been expecting my call. She would be pleased if I would have tea at their home, perhaps the following day at four o'clock? I thanked her and accepted the invitation.

The family lived in one of the old brownstone houses on the upper East Side of the city. The exterior had been kept up with great care and fastidiousness. The door was highly polished, the brass trim shining. The house was located on a beautiful old street and seemed to have preserved the essence of the days when these lovely old mansions were erected. I opened the wrought iron gate, walked up the steps, and rang the door chimes. Through the closed door I could hear muffled screams. "No lock door! No lock door! No! No! No!" The voice trailed off into silence. Apparently, Dibs was not going to join us for tea. A uniformed maid opened the door. I introduced myself. She invited me into the drawing room. The maid was a very trim, serious woman who looked as though she could have been with the family for many years. She was remote, precise, formal. I wondered if she ever smiled—or even felt that there was anything light and amusing in the world. If so, she was well disciplined and concealed any individual identity and spontaneity.

Dibs' mother greeted me graciously, but seriously. We made the usual introductory remarks about the weather and how nice it was to have this opportunity to visit with one another. The house was beautifully and precisely furnished. The drawing room didn't look as though a child had ever spent five minutes there. In fact, there were no signs that anyone really *lived* in this house.

Tea was brought in. The service was beautiful. She didn't waste much time structuring the situation.

"I understand that you have been called in as a consultant to study Dibs," she said. "It is very kind of you to undertake this assignment. And I want you to know that we do not expect any miracle. We have accepted the tragedy of Dibs. I know something about your professional reputation and have great respect for research into all sciences—including the science of human behavior. We do not expect any changes in Dibs; but, if in studying this child, you can advance the understanding of human behavior even a little, we are more than willing to cooperate."

It was incredible. Here she was, in the best scientific manner, offering me some data to study. Not a child in trouble. Not her son. Some raw data. And she made it very clear that she did not expect any changes in the data. At least, no changes for the better. I listened as she told me very briefly the vital statistics of Dibs. His date of birth. The slow progress. The obvious retardation. The possibility of organic involvement. She sat in her chair, almost without moving. Tense. Terribly controlled. Her face was very pale. Her grey hair was parted in the middle and pulled back into a knot at the nape of her neck. Her eyes were light blue. Her lips were thinned into line. Occasionally, she bit her lip nervously. Her dress was steel grey, classically simple. In a cold way, she was a very handsome woman. It would be difficult to guess her age. She looked as though she was well up in her fifties, but she could have been much younger. She had precise, intelligent speech. She seemed to be putting up a brave front; but, in all probability, she was as deeply and tragically unhappy as Dibs.

Then she asked me if I would study Dibs here in his playroom upstairs—in the back.

"It is upstairs—in the rear of the house," she said.

"No one would ever interrupt or bother you there. He has many toys. And we would be glad to get any other materials you might want or need."

"No thank you," I said. "It will be better if I see him in the playroom at the Child Guidance Center. The sessions will be once a week for an hour."

This was obviously a disturbing arrangement. She tried again. "He has many lovely toys in his room. We would be pleased to pay you a higher fee if you would come here."

"I'm sorry, but I couldn't do it," I told her. "And there will be no fee at all."

"Oh, but we can well afford to pay," she said, quickly. "I insist that we pay you a fee for this study."

"That is very kind of you," I said. "But there will be no fee. All I ask is that you see to it that he gets to the Center on time and attends regularly—unless, of course, he should be ill. And I would like your permission in writing to record fully all the interviews for our study. And I will give you a written statement that in the event this material is ever used for teaching or reporting or publication in any form, all identifying information will be disguised so completely that no one will ever know or be able to guess the true identity of Dibs."

I handed her the statement that had been drawn up before this meeting. She studied it carefully.

"Very well," she said, finally. "Shall I keep this?"

"Yes. And will you and your husband sign this statement, giving us your consent to record fully all the interviews, with the stipulation that the material will be completely disguised if it is ever reported?"

She took this paper and studied it very carefully. "May I keep this and discuss it with my husband and mail it to you, if we decide to go through with this?"

"Certainly, you may," I said. "I would appreciate it if you would let me know one way or the other as soon as you decide."

She held the slip of paper gingerly. She moistened her lips. This was certainly a far cry from the usual initial interview with a mother. I felt as uncomfortable as she probably did, making a deal out of this business of seeing her child in the playroom. But I felt that this was a long chance that I had to take—or Dibs would not come to the Center.

"I'll let you know as soon as we decide," she said.

My heart sank a little. She could use this as a way out. But if she did agree to it, she committed herself to seeing it through. I was certain that if they did sign it, they would keep their part of the bargain. If they did not accept this much responsibility, we could not depend upon the necessary regular attendance.

After a long pause, she said, "I don't understand why, when a family is able to pay a substantial fee so that you could see another child whose parents may not be able to pay, you refuse a fee."

"Because my work is primarily in research to increase our understanding of children," I explained. "I am paid a salary for the work I do. This eliminates the factor of ability to pay or to feel that you are receiving a service some pay for and some do not. If you care to make a research contribution to the Center quite apart from any tie-in with this particular case, that is entirely up to you. Research is primarily financed in that manner."

"I see," she said. "But I would still be willing to pay you."

"I'm sure you would," I told her. "And I appreciate your concern about this. However, I can only see Dibs on these conditions."

I had done it now. I was way out on the limb and she could cut it off with the speed of an electric saw. I felt strongly that if we weathered this little controversy, we would have achieved something of importance in building up the necessary initial responsibility for the mother. She had probably often been able to pay her way out of taking this much involved responsibility for Dibs. I decided that it was important to eliminate this factor as best I could at this time.

She was very quiet for a few minutes. Her hands were

clasped tightly in her lap. She was looking down at them. Suddenly, I remembered Dibs, throwing himself face down, prone on the floor—rigid, quiet. Again, I thought that she was as sad and remote as her son.

Finally she glanced at me, looked away quickly, avoided my eyes. "I must tell you this," she said. "I can only refer you to the school for any more details of Dibs' case history. There is nothing more that I can add. And I will not be able to come in for any interviews myself. If that is one of your conditions, we will forget the whole arrangement right now. There is nothing more that I can add. It is a tragedy—a great tragedy. But Dibs? Well, he is just mentally retarded. He was born that way. But I cannot come in for any interviews or questioning." She glanced at me again. She looked terrified at the thought of any interviewing for herself.

"I understand," I said. "I'll respect your wishes in this matter. But, I would like to say this. If at any time at all you ever do want to talk to me about Dibs, feel free to get in touch with me. But I will leave that entirely up to you."

She seemed to relax a little.

"My husband is not willing to come in, either," she said.

"That's all right," I said. "Whatever you decide."

"When I bring him to the Center, I won't be able to stay there and wait for him. I'll have to come back when the hour is up," she added.

"That will be all right," I assured her. "You may bring him over and leave him there, then pick him up after the hour is over. Or you may send him over with someone else, if you prefer."

"Thank you," she said. Then after another very long pause, she added "I appreciate your understanding."

We finished our tea. We talked about a few more non-essentials. Dorothy was mentioned only as a vital statistic and "a perfect child." Dibs' mother had shown more fear, anxiety, and panic in this interview than Dibs had shown in his first session. There would be nothing gained by trying to persuade her to come in for some help for herself. It was too much of a threat to her. And too risky. Chances are, we would only lose Dibs. Besides, I had a strong feeling that Dibs would be far more responsive than his mother ever could be. Dibs had protested the locking of doors, but some very important doors in her life had already been securely locked. It was almost too late for her to protest. As a matter of fact, in this brief interview she had been desperately trying to lock another door.

As I took my departure, she came to the door with me.

"You're sure you wouldn't rather see him in his playroom?" she asked. "He has so many nice toys. And we would buy anything else that you might want. Anything."

She was really desperate. I felt a twinge of sympathy for her. I thanked her for her offer, but again told her that I could only see him in the playroom at the Center.

"I will let you know as soon as we decide," she said, with a slight wave of the paper she held.

"Thank you," I said. I left. Walking down the street to my car, I felt the oppressive weight of that troubled family. I thought of Dibs and his beautifully equipped playoom. I did not have to enter that playroom to be reasonably certain that everything money could buy was there. And I was absolutely certain that there was a solid, highly polished door, too. And a sturdy lock that was too often locked securely.

I wondered what she would be able to add to the story of Dibs if she should ever decide to tell it. Certainly, there were no glib answers to explain the dynamics of the family relationships here. What must this woman really think and feel about Dibs and the part she played in his young life to be so terrorized at the prospect of being interviewed and questioned about the situation?

I wondered whether I had handled the situation in the most fruitful way—or whether I had only put on pressure that might cause her to back away from the study of this child. I wondered what decision she and her husband might make. Would they consent to the arrangements we had discussed? Would I ever see Dibs again? And if I did, what would grow out of the experience?

Chapter Four

A PERIOD OF SEVERAL WEEKS FOLLOWED during which I heard not one word from Dibs' mother. I called the school and asked the headmistress if she had heard anything from the parents. She said she had not heard from them either. I inquired about Dibs. She said that things were about the same as usual. Dibs had been attending school regularly. They were, more or less, just standing by, hoping that the play sessions would soon begin.

Then one morning I received the signed release slip from the parents, giving me permission to record the sessions. There was a brief note stating their willingness to cooperate in our study of the child and suggesting that I call them and arrange for the weekly appointments with Dibs.

I scheduled the interview for the following Thursday afternoon in the playroom at the Center. I asked my secretary to call Dibs' mother and ask if the time was convenient. She said the time was satisfactory and that she would bring him over to the Center.

Several of us sighed with relief. Apparently this family did not make such decisions lightly. One could only speculate on the significance of the delay in following through on the play sessions and imagine the turmoil and misgivings the parents had undergone as they studied the next move they might make. And what of Dibs in the meantime? Had they been taking thoughtful looks in his direction, trying to size up the possible outcomes of any attempt at evaluation of his abilities? In all likelihood, they had been carefully weighing all the angles involved in this venture. It had been a real temptation to call the mother and urge her to bring Dibs in—or ask if they had made any decision. I had not done so because I felt that we had nothing to gain by trying to force a decision (if one had not already been made) and much to lose, if they were still considering what they might ultimately do. It had been a long and frustrating wait.

Dibs arrived at the Center promptly with his mother. She told the receptionist she would return for him in one hour and left him in the waiting room. I went in to greet him. He was standing on the spot where his mother had left him, wearing his coat, hat, mittens, and boots.

I walked up to him. "Good afternoon, Dibs,' I said. "It is good to see you again. Let's go back to the playroom. It's at the end of this hall."

Dibs reached out and silently took my hand. We walked down the hall to the playroom.

"This is another playroom," I said to him. "It is something like the one in your school where I saw you several weeks ago."

"That's right," he said haltingly.

This playroom was on the ground floor. The room was bright with sunshine. It was a more attractive room than the other one, but the equipment was essentially the same. The windows looked out over a parking lot and on the other side of the lot was a large grey stone church.

When we got into the playroom, Dibs walked slowly around, touching the materials, naming the items with the same questioning inflection he had used on the first visit to the other playroom.

"Sandbox? Easel? Chair? Paint? Car? Doll? Doll house?" Every item he touched, he named in that manner. Then he varied it a little. "Is this a car? This is a car. Is this sand? This is sand. Is this paint? It is paint."

After he had completed the first circuit of the room, I said, "Yes. There are many different things in this room, aren't there? And you have touched and named most of them."

"That's right," he said, softly.

I didn't want to rush him. Give him time to look around and explore. Every child needs time to explore his world in his own way.

He stopped in the middle of the room.

"I say, Dibs! Would you like to take off your hat and coat?" I asked him after a while.

"That's right," he said. "You take off your hat and coat, Dibs. You take off your hat. You take off your coat, Dibs." He made no motion to do anything about it.

"Then you would like to take off your coat and hat?" I asked. "All right, Dibs. Go ahead. Take them off."

"Take off mittens and boots, too," he said.

"All right," I replied. "Take off your mittens and your boots, too, if you want to."

"That's right," he said, almost in a whisper. He stood there, plucking idly and restlessly at his coat sleeves. He began to whimper. He stood in front of me, hanging his head, whimpering.

"You would like to take them off, but you want me to help you? Is that it?" I asked.

"That's right," he said. There was a sob in his voice as he replied.

I sat down on a little chair and said, "All right, Dibs. If you want me to help you take off your coat and hat, come over here and I will help you." This, too, was done with a purpose in mind. I offered to help him, but sat down in such a location in the room that in order to get the help he would have to take a few steps of his own for it.

He walked haltingly toward me. "Boots, too," he said, huskily.

"All right. We'll take off the boots, too," I said.

"And mittens," he said, holding out his hands.

"All right. And the mittens, too," I replied. I helped him off with his mittens, hat, coat, boots. I put the mittens in his coat pocket, handed him his coat and hat. He dropped them on the floor. I picked them up and hung them on the doorknob.

"Let's put them here until it is time to go," I said. "We

have an hour to spend together in this room, then it will be time for you to go home again."

He did not reply. He walked over to the easel and looked at the paints. He stood there for a long time. Then he named the colors on the easel. Slowly he re-arranged them. He placed the red, yellow, and blue on the shelf of the easel. Carefully, he moved them apart and in the appropriate spaces added other colors to give the six full-strength colors of the spectrum. Then he set the tertiary color in correct places, added the black and white, and had on the edge of the easel the full color and color value scale. He did this silently, slowly, carefully.

When he had them all lined up in order, he picked up one of the jars and examined it. He looked into the jar, stirred the paint with the brush in the jar, held it up to the light, ran his fingers lightly over the label.

"Favor Ruhl paints," he said. "Red. Favor Ruhl paints. Yellow. Favor Ruhl paints. Blue. Favor Ruhl paints. Black."

This was a partial answer to one question. He was obviously reading the labels. They were indeed, Favor Ruhl paints. And the colors were correctly arranged and named.

"Well," I said. "So you can read the labels on the paint jars. And you know all the names of the colors."

"That's right," he said haltingly.

Then he sat down at the table and reached for the box of crayons. He read the name on the box. Then he took out the red crayon and printed in neat, block letters, "RED." He did the same with all the other colors and used them in the same ordered, full-colored sequence, in a circle. As he printed them out he spelled them, naming each letter as he printed it.

I watched him. I tried to respond verbally to him in recognition of his attempt to communicate with me in this activity. "You are going to spell out the names of each color and print it in that color. Is that correct? I see. R-E-D spells red, doesn't it?"

"That's right," he said, slowly, haltingly.

"And you are making a color wheel, aren't you?"

"That's right," he muttered.

He picked up the box of watercolors. He read the trade name on the box. He dabbed blotches of color on a piece of drawing paper in the same deliberate, rigid sequence.

I attempted to keep my comments in line with his activity, trying not to say anything that would indicate any desire on my part that he do any particular thing, but rather to communicate, understandingly and simply, recognition in line with his frame of reference. I wanted him to lead the way. I would follow. I wanted to let him know from the beginning that he would set the pace in that room and that I would recognize his efforts at two-way communication with some concrete reality basis of a shared experience between the two of us. I didn't want to go overboard and exclaim about his ability to do all these things. Obviously he could do these things. When the initiative is left up to the individual, he will select the ground upon which he feels his greatest security. Any exclamation of surprise or praise might be interpreted by him as the direction he must take. It might close off any other areas of exploration that might be far more important for him. All people proceed with a caution that will protect the integrity of their personality. We were getting acquainted. These *things* Dibs mentioned, objects in this room that were not involved with any serious affect, were the only shared ingredients at this point for communication between us. To Dibs these were safe concepts.

Occasionally he would glance at me, but when our eyes met, he would immediately look away.

Certainly his beginning activities were a revelation. Hedda had good reason for her faith in Dibs. He was, indeed, not only on the verge of coming through, but actually emerging. Whatever his problems were, we could discard the label of mental retardation.

He climbed into the sandbox. He lined up the soldiers, matching the pairs two by two. The sand sifted into his shoes. He glanced at me, pointed to his shoes, whimpered.

"What is it?" I asked. "Is the sand getting into your shoes?"

He nodded his head.

"If you want to take off your shoes, go ahead," I said.

"That's right," he replied, huskily. But he did not take them off. Instead, he sat there, staring down at his shoes, whimpering. I waited. Finally, he spoke. "You will take your shoes off," he said, speaking with great effort.

"You want them off, but you want me to help you," I replied. "Is that it?"

He nodded his head. I gave the requested assistance, untied his shoe laces and removed his shoes. He very gingerly touched the sand with his feet and in a few minutes was ready to get out.

He walked over to the table and looked at the blocks. Then slowly, deliberately, he placed one on top of the other. The stack of blocks wavered and fell over. He clasped his hands together.

"Miss A!" he cried, giving me the name he used thereafter when he referred to me. "Help me. Quick."

"You really like to have me help you, don't you?" I commented.

"That's right," he said. He shot another fleeting glance in my direction.

"Well, what do you want me to do?" I asked him. "You tell me, Dibs."

He stood beside the table, looking down at the blocks, his hands still clasped tightly against his chest.

Dibs was silent. So was I.

What was he thinking? What was he seeking? What would be most helpful for Dibs now? I wanted to communicate an honest attempt to understand him. I didn't know what he was really after. He probably didn't know, either, at this point in our developing relationship. Certainly, it was not appropriate to probe into his private world and try to drag out answers. If I could get across to Dibs my confidence in him as a person who had good reasons for everything he did, and if I could convey the concept that there were no hidden answers for him to guess, no con-

cealed standards of behavior or expression that were not
openly stated, no pressure for him to read my mind and
come up with a solution that I had already decided upon,
no rush to do everything today—then, perhaps, Dibs
would catch more and more of a feeling of security and of
the rightness of his own reactions so he could clarify,
understand, and accept them. This would take time, real
effort, great patience on the part of both of us. And it
must at all times be basically and fundamentally honest.

He reached out suddenly, took a small block in each
hand and crashed them together. "A wreck," he said.

"Oh," I said. "That was a wreck?"

"That's right," he replied. "A wreck!"

A truck drove into the parking lot and stopped beside
the open window. Dibs went over to the window and
started to close it. It was very hot in the room with the
window open, but he cranked the handle to close the
window.

"Close window," he said.

"You want to close the window?" I asked. "But it is
very hot in here today with the window open."

"That's right," Dibs answered. "You will close it,
Dibs."

"Oh," I said. "You want it closed, anyway."

"That's right," he said. "Dibs close it!" He spoke with
firmness.

"You really know what you want, don't you?" I commented.

He dabbed clumsily at his tear-streaked face. It would
have been so easy to take him in my arms and console
him, to extend the hour, to try overtly to give him a
demonstration of affection and sympathy. But of what
value would it have been to add additional emotional
problems to this child's life? He *did* have to go back to his
home no matter how he felt about it. To avoid facing this
reality factor would not help him. He needed to develop
strength to cope with his world, but that strength had to
come from within him and he had to experience personally his ability to cope with his world as it was. Any

meaningful changes for Dibs would have to come from within him. We could not hope to make over his external world.

Finally, he was dressed to leave. He took my hand and walked down the hall with me to the reception room. His mother stood there waiting for him, looking very much like Dibs—uncomfortable, ill at ease, not at all sure of herself or of the situation. When Dibs saw her, he threw himself face down on the floor and kicked and screamed his protest. I said goodbye to him, told his mother I would see him next week, and left them. There was a fuss in the waiting room while his mother tried to get him to leave. She was embarrassed and aggravated by his behavior.

I wasn't happy about this development, but I didn't know what to do other than to leave them there to work it out in their own way. It seemed to me that if I stayed and either looked on or interfered it would only confuse and complicate the situation. I did not want to seem to be lining up either for or against Dibs or his mother. I did not want to do anything that might imply criticism of their behavior—or to be either supportive or rejecting of mother or child. So it seemed that to leave the scene without getting personally involved would be a better procedure.

Chapter Five

THE FOLLOWING WEEK Dibs returned to the Center. He was exceedingly prompt for his appointment. I was in my office when the receptionist buzzed the signal that announced Dibs' arrival. I walked down to the reception room at once. There stood Dibs, just inside the door. His mother had brought him into the reception room, spoken briefly to the receptionist, and departed.

"Good afternoon, Dibs," I said, as I walked up to him. He did not reply. He stood there, eyes downcast.

"Let's go back to the playroom," I said, holding out my hand to him. He took my hand and walked down the hall to the playroom. I stood aside for Dibs to enter. He started to go into the room, but suddenly pulled back and grasped the edge of the door. There was a reversible sign on the door. Dibs reached up and took the card out of the holder.

"Do not disturb," he read. He turned the sign and looked at the words on the other side. "Play," he read. He tapped the second word with his finger several times. This was a new word to him. Therapy. He studied it carefully. "The rapy," he said.

"It is pronounced *therapy*," I said, giving him the correct pronunciation.

"Play therapy room?" he said.

"Yes," I replied.

"Play therapy room," he said again. Then he entered the playroom and closed the door behind us. "You will take off your hat and coat," he said.

I looked at him. I knew he was referring to himself, but

48

was using the second person pronoun. Dibs seldom had been heard to refer to himself as "I."

"You want me to take *my* hat and coat off?" I asked him.

"That's right," he said.

"But *I* don't have a hat and coat on," I told him. Dibs looked at me.

"You will take your hat and coat off," he said, pulling at his coat.

"Do you want me to help you take off your hat and coat? Is that it?" I asked him. I had hoped to focus his attention on the pronoun *I*, but this was a confusing and complicated problem.

"That's right," Dibs said.

"I'll help you," I said. And I did, with more help from him this time. I held out the hat and coat toward him after I had taken them off.

He glanced at me, took the coat and hat, and walked toward the door with them. "You will hang them here," he said, hanging them on the doorknob.

"I hung them there last week," I said. "You will hang them up today."

"That's right," he replied.

He sat down on the edge of the sandbox and again matched the toy soldiers in pairs and lined them up. Then he went over to the doll house and re-arranged the furniture in it. "Where's the door? Where's the door?" he asked, pointing to the open front of the doll house.

"I think it is inside the cupboard over there," I said.

Dibs went over to the cupboard and got out the front panel of the doll house. As he walked around the doll house, he hit it with the front wall of the house and one of the partitions fell down. He straightened it, fitted it into its correct groove. Then he tried to attach the panel, on which was painted the door and windows. It was difficult to do. He tried several times and each time failed to connect the hooks. He whimpered.

"Lock it up," he muttered. "Lock it up."

"Do you want the house locked up?" I asked.

"Locked up," he replied. He tried again. This time he succeeded. "There it is," he announced. "Locked tight."

"I see. You got it on and locked it," I said.

Dibs looked at me. He gave me a brief, fleeting smile. *"I* did," he said, falteringly.

"You really did. And by yourself, too," I commented. He grinned. He seemed very pleased with himself.

He went around to the back of the doll house and closed all the shutters on the windows. "All shut," he said. "All locked and shut. All closed and locked."

"Yes. I see they are," I said.

He dropped down on his hands and knees and looked at the bottom part of the house. There were two doors hinged on this section of the house. He opened these doors. "There," he said. "That's basement. Take these out. Walls, more walls and partitions. Walls without doors." In the bottom were stored other partitions and more doll house furniture.

"Make a doorknob," he said. He reached up, took my pencil, and very carefully drew a doorknob on the door of the doll house.

"Do you think there ought to be a doorknob on the door?" I asked him.

"That's right," he muttered. He drew a lock on the door. "Got a lock on it now, too."

"Yes, I see. You've put a doorknob and a lock on that door."

"A lock that locks tight with a key," he said. "And high, hard walls. And a door. A locked door."

"I see," I commented.

The house wobbled a little as Dibs touched it. He examined it. He took out one of the partitions and tried to fit it under the corner of the house to steady it. After trying to insert the partition under two of the corners, he pushed it under the third corner and the house no longer wobbled.

"There," he said. "Doesn't wobble any more. No rock and no wobble, now."

He raised up a part of the hinged roof and moved some

of the furniture. The partition slid out of position and the house began to wobble again. Dibs stepped back and looked at it. "Miss A, put some wheels on it, then it will no longer wobble and rock," he said.

"Do you think that would solve the problem?" I asked.

"It would," he replied. "It would, indeed."

So Dibs obviously had many words in his unused vocabulary. He could observe and define problems. He could solve these problems. Why had he drawn a lock on the door of the doll house? The locked doors in his life had certainly made an impression on Dibs.

He walked to the sandbox and climbed in. He picked out some of the toy soldiers that were scattered throughout the sand. He examined each soldier as he picked it up. "Dibs got some for Christmas like this," he said, gesturing toward me with one of them.

"Did you get some toy soldiers like that for Christmas?" I repeated.

"Yes. Exactly like them," he replied. "Well, not exactly. But the same kind. For Christmas. These have guns in their hands. These are the guns right here. They shoot. Guns, real guns, shoot. This one carries his gun over his shoulder. This one has it out in shooting position. Look. Here are four that are very much alike. And here are four more. Here are three with guns pointed out this way. And here is one other like that. Four and four are eight. Add three and one more and that is twelve."

"I see," I said, watching as he grouped the soldiers. "You can add up the groups of soldiers and get the correct answer."

"That's right," Dibs said. Then, haltingly, he added, "I . . . I . . . *I* can."

"Yes, you can, Dibs," I said.

"These two men are with flags," he said, indicating two other figures. He lined them all up along the edge of the sandbox. "These all have guns," he said. "They are shooting their guns. But they have their backs this way," he added.

"Do you mean they are all shooting in the same direction?" I asked, pointing rather vaguely in the direction of the soldiers.

Dibs looked at me. He looked down at the soldiers. He hung his head. "They are not shooting—*at you*," he said gruffly.

"I understand," I said. "They are not shooting at me."

"That's right," he said.

He dragged his hand through the sand and found some more toy soldiers. He picked them out and lined them up. He wiggled his feet with his shoes on down into the sand.

"Take off shoes," he said suddenly. He untied his shoe laces and removed his shoes. Then he re-arranged the soldiers.

"There you are," he said. "They are all lined up together. They are all together."

He selected three soldiers, and stood them up in a row. Carefully, deliberately, he pushed each one down into the sand. The third one did not go down far enough to satisfy him. He extracted that one and pushed it far down under the sand, picked up a handful of sand, and sifted it down on top of the buried soldiers.

"He is gone!" Dibs announced.

"You got rid of him, didn't you?" I commented.

"That's right," said Dibs. He shoveled the sand into a bucket and dumped a bucketful of sand down on the buried soldiers.

The chimes in the church on the other side of the parking lot began to play, then to strike the hour. Dibs stopped his activity.

"Listen," he said. "One. Two. Three. Four. That's four o'clock."

"Yes. It is four o'clock. It will soon be time for you to go home," I said.

Dibs ignored my remark. He got out of the sandbox and hurried over to the table. He looked at the jars of finger paint. "What is this?" he asked.

"That is finger paint," I told him.

"Finger paint? How?"

I showed him how to use the finger paint. "First, wet

the paper. Then put some of the paint on the paper. Then spread it around with your fingers, or your hands. Like this. Any way you want to use it, Dibs."

He listened. He watched the very brief demonstration.

"Finger paints?" he asked.

"Yes. Finger paint."

He dipped a very tentative finger down over the red paint. "Spread it 'round and 'round," he said. But he could not bear to touch the paint. He circled his hands closely over the wet paper. Then he picked up a wooden spatula, dipped that in the paint, and spread it around on the paper.

"I think this is finger paint," he said. "Yes. You said it is finger paint. Spread it around and around with your fingers." Again he touched the paint with his fingers. "Oh, wipe it off," he said.

I handed him a paper towel. He wiped the paint off.

"Don't you like to get the paint on your hands?" I asked.

"It is messy paint," he said. "Messy, smeary paint."

He picked up the jar and read the label. "This is the red finger paint," he announced. "Red." He put the jar down on the table and circled the outstretched palms of his hands around above the paint and paper, very close to it but not touching it. Quickly, he touched the paint with the tip of his fingers.

"Spread it on," he said. "Take the red paint, Dibs, and spread it on. Spread it on one finger, two fingers, three fingers. First the red. Then the yellow. Then the blue. Put it on in order."

"You would sort of like to try it?" I asked.

"These are all the signs of what it says it is," Dibs said, looking up at me and then pointing to the labels on the jars.

"Yes. Those are the directions."

He dipped his fingers in the paint again. "Oh, take it off," he said. He picked up another paper towel and wiped the paint off vigorously.

"You would sort of like to do it, and then again, you don't like it," I commented.

"Now those crayons are different," Dibs said. "The American Crayon Company makes those. And this is the Shaw Finger Paint. The watercolors are made by Prang."

"Yes," I said.

"These are finger paints," Dibs said. He dipped his fingers into the yellow paint and slowly, deliberately, spread it over each of his fingers. Then he wiped it off with the paper towels. Next he dipped his fingers into the blue paint. He put his hand down on the paper and bent over, very absorbed in what he was doing. He spread the paint carefully over each finger. "There," he said triumphantly, holding out his hands. "Look."

"You really did it that time, didn't you?" I remarked.

"Look," he said. "Fingers all full of blue finger paint." He looked at his hands. "Fingers all blue, now. Now they are all green," he said, as he changed the color. "First, I made them red," he said. "Then yellow. Then blue. Then green. Then brown. I put it on each finger. I wiped it off. Cleaned off each color and made it another color. So this is finger paint! Oh, come away, Dibs. It is a very silly kind of paint. Come away!" He wiped the paint off his fingers and tossed the paper towels into the waste basket. He shook his head in disgust.

"Finger paints," he said. "They are not of interest to me. I will paint a picture."

"Think you would rather paint a picture?" I said.

"Yes," he replied. "With the watercolor."

"There are only five minutes left," I said. "Do you think you could paint a picture in five minutes?"

"Dibs will paint," he announced. He got the box of paints. "Where is water?" he asked.

I pointed to the sink. He filled a paint pan with water.

"You will have time to paint this one picture," I said. "Then it will be time to go."

This was a risky statement. He might extend the time to paint this one picture as long as he wanted to, since the time limit had with my word become flexible. Since I meant "five more minutes," I should have held to that limit and not complicated the situation by introducing a second element.

However, Dibs ignored my statement. "The paint runs," he said. "I'll blot it with the paper towel. That will dry it. This will be a picture." Using quick, deft strokes, he started with the red paint and made on the paper what seemed at first to be various shaped blobs of color, placing them at various spots on the paper, adding each color in the same sequence as on color wheels. As he added more colors the picture emerged. When he had completed it, he had a painting of a house, a tree, sky, grass, flowers, the sun. All the colors were used. There was in the finished painting relationships, form, and meaning.

"This is. . . . This is. . . ." He was stammering and fumbling with the brush, hanging his head, suddenly appearing to be very shy. "This is Miss A's house," he said. "Miss A, I'll give you this house."

"You want to give me that, do you?" I said, gesturing toward his painting. He nodded. The purpose of this response, rather than an expression of thank you's and praise, was to keep our communication open and to slow it down. Then, if he wanted to, he could add more of his thoughts and feelings and not be abruptly cut off by my response and involvement and values or standards of behavior.

Dibs picked up the pencil and painstakingly drew a lock on the door. He drew some small, barred windows down low on the house. There was one big window that he had colored bright yellow. He had painted a pot of red flowers in that window. It was quite an amazing bit of creative art and had been accomplished in a very unique way.

He looked at me. His eyes were bright blue. The expression on his face was one of unhappiness and fear. He pointed to the door in the picture. "It's got a lock on it," he said. "It locks fast with a key. It's got a basement that is dark."

I looked at his painting, then I looked at him. "So I

see," I commented. "This house, too, has a lock and a dark basement."

He stared at the house. He touched the lock on the door. He looked at me.

"This house is for you," he said. He was twisting his fingers together. "This is your house, now," he added. He took a deep breath. Then he added with great effort, "This house has a playroom, too." He pointed to the bright yellow window and the red flowers in the pot in that window.

"Oh, yes. I see. That is the playroom window, isn't it?"

Dibs nodded. "That's right," he said.

He walked over to the sink and emptied the paint water. He turned the water on full force. The church chimes began to play again.

"Listen, Dibs," I said. "It is time to go now. Do you hear the chimes?"

Dibs ignored my remark. "The brown makes the water brown and the orange paint makes the water orange," he said.

"Yes, they do," I replied. I knew that he had heard my statement about the time. I did not intend to act as though I thought he had not heard me.

"This is H-O-T water. Hot," he said. "And C-O-L-D water. Cold. Hot. Cold. On. Off. On. Off."

"Do you find the hot and cold water interesting, too, now?" I asked.

"That's right," he said.

"But what did I tell you about our time, Dibs?" I asked.

He twisted his hands together and turned around toward me, looking very miserable and unhappy. "Miss A say it paint one picture of a house and then it leave you," he said, huskily. I noted how confused his language had become. Here was a child very capable of great intellectual achievement, whose abilities were dominated by his emotional disturbance.

. ."That is what I said, Dibs," I replied quietly. "And you have finished painting the picture and it is time to go."

"I'll need some more grass here and some flowers," he said suddenly.

"There is no more time for that," I said. "Our time is up for today."

Dibs walked over to the doll house. "I'll have to fix the house. I'll have to close it up," he said.

"You can think of several things to do so you won't have to go home, can't you? But your time is up now, Dibs, and you will have to go home now."

"No. Wait. Wait," Dibs cried out.

"I know you don't want to go, Dibs. But our time is up for today."

"No go now," he sobbed. "No go now. No go ever."

"It makes you unhappy when I say you have to leave, doesn't it, Dibs? But you may come back again next week. Next Thursday."

I picked up his hat, coat, and boots. Dibs sat down on the little chair by the table. He eyed me tearfully as I put his cap on his head.

Suddenly, he brightened up. "Friday?" he asked. "Come back Friday?"

"You will come back next Thursday," I said. "Because Thursday is the day you come to the playroom."

Dibs suddenly stood up. "No!" he shouted. "Dibs no go out of here. Dibs no go home. Not never!"

"I know you don't want to go, Dibs. But you and I only have one hour every week to spend together here in this playroom. And when that hour is over, no matter how you feel about it, no matter how I feel about it, no matter how anybody feels about it, it is over for that day and we both leave the playroom. *Now* it is time for us to go. In fact, it is a little past the time."

"Cannot paint another picture?" Dibs asked me, tears streaming down his face.

"Not today," I told him.

"A picture for you?" he asked. "One more picture I paint just for you?"

"No. Our time is up for today." I said.

He was standing in front of me. I held his coat for him.

"Come on, Dibs. Put your arms into your coat sleeves."
He did. "Now sit down while I put your boots on."

He sat down muttering "No go home. No want to go
home. No *feel* like going home."

"I know how you *feel*," I told him.

A child gets his feelings of security from predictable
and consistent and realistic limitations. I had hoped to
help Dibs differentiate between his *feelings* and his actions. He seemed to have achieved a bit of this. I also
hoped to communicate to him the fact that this one hour
was only a part of his existence, that it could not and
should not take precedence over all other relationships
and experiences, that all the time between the weekly
sessions was important, too. The value of any successful
therapeutic experience, in my opinion, depends upon the
balance that is maintained between what the individual
brings into the sessions and what he takes out. If the
therapy becomes the predominant and controlling influence in the individual's daily life, then I would have
serious doubts as to its effectiveness. I wanted Dibs to feel
that he had the responsibility to take away with him his
increasing ability to assume responsibility for himself and
thus gain his psychological independence.

As I put on his boots, I glanced up at him. He had
reached across the table and picked up the nursing bottle
which contained water. He was sucking on it like a small
baby. Finally, the boots were on.

"Now, then," I said. "They are on."

"Put tops on paint jars?" he asked, taking one more
chance.

"Not now," I said.

"They will dry up?" he said.

"If the tops were left off, they would," I replied. "I'll
put the tops on later."

"Put the lids on the finger paints?" he asked.

"Yes. That will be done, too."

"Clean the brushes?"

"Yes."

Dibs sighed. He had apparently exhausted his resources.

He stood up and walked out the door. Just outside the door, he stopped abruptly, reached up and turned the sign on the door from *Do Not Disturb* to *Play Therapy Room*. He patted the door. "Our playroom," he said. He walked down the hall to the reception room and left with his surprised mother without a fuss.

Chapter Six

WHEN DIBS ENTERED THE PLAYROOM the following Thursday, he went to the table and looked at the jars of finger paint. He picked up each jar, checked the lids, replaced them in the long, narrow box. Lids are on, he commented.

"Yes. I remembered to fix them," I said.

"So I see," Dibs remarked.

He picked up the nursing bottle. "I want to suck it," he said. He stood there, sucking on the nipple, looking at me. Then he put the bottle down on the table.

"Take off your clothes," he said. He unbuttoned his coat, removed it without assistance, and hung it on the doorknob. He took off his hat and put it on the chair beside the door.

He went over to the doll house and opened all the windows. "Look," he said. "All the windows are open. Now, I'll shut them all up." He picked up the front of the house, suddenly changed his mind, dropped it on the floor, and returned to the table and reached for the nursing bottle.

"I'll suck on the bottle," he announced.

"Do you like to suck on the bottle?" I asked—again, more to keep open the channel of communication than to add any enlightenment to the conversation.

"That's right," he said. He sucked on the bottle in silence for a long time, watching me as he did. Then he put down the bottle, walked over to the cupboard, opened the doors, and looked in.

He got out the empty box that had contained some of the small blocks. "The Cubical Counting Blocks fit in here," he said. He fitted several of the blocks into the box. "See?" he said. "This is the box. This is what it says they are." He pointed to the name on the lid.

"Yes, I know," I remarked. I was interested in the manner in which Dibs had been displaying his ability to read, count, solve problems. It seemed to me that whenever he approached any kind of emotional reference he retreated to a demonstration of his ability to read. Perhaps he felt safer in manipulating intellectual concepts about *things*, rather than probing any deeper into feelings about himself that he could not accept with ease. Perhaps this was a brief bit of evidence of some conflict he had between expectations of his behavior and his own striving to be himself—sometimes very capable, sometimes a baby. He had taken this retreat on several occasions in the playroom. Perhaps he felt that his intellectual abilities were the only part of him that was valued by others. Why, then, would he have worked so strenuously to conceal his capacities at school and at home? Could it be because he desired above all things to be a person in his own right, respected and loved for *all* his qualities? How could a child have concealed so well this wealth of intellectual substance that was so close beneath the surface of his resistive external behavior? How had he learned all these skills? He could read far beyond his years. How had he achieved this without first showing evidence of a meaningful, verbal language? The astuteness and strength of this child were incredible. How could he have concealed this ability from his family, if, indeed, he had done so?

It would be extremely interesting to be able to fill in these gaps in our understanding; but we had made an agreement, his mother and I, that there would be no probing. I could only hope that she would some day feel secure enough within herself to share with me what she knew about Dibs' development. Besides, it was evident that intellectual achievement without the attendant emotional and social maturity was not enough. Was this the reason for the dissatisfaction in Dibs by his family? Or had his mother felt an uneasiness and fear of Dibs because she could not understand him?

In all probability there were many very complicated reasons why the relationship between Dibs and his family was so deficient. It would be very helpful to know more of the answers to some of the questions that raced through my mind as I watched Dibs fluctuate between bottle-sucking, infantile behavior, and a precise, almost compulsive intellectual display.

Dibs was sitting on the chair, sucking contentedly on the nursing bottle, relaxed, looking steadily at me. I wondered what unanswered questions raced through his mind. Suddenly, he sat up straight, removed the nipple, drank from the bottle, spilled some on the floor as he drank.

He pointed to the two buzzers on the wall. "That's doorbells," he said.

"Yes. Like doorbells," I answered.

He picked up the nipple, chewed and sucked on it, looking steadily at me. Finally, he motioned toward my feet. I was wearing red toe-rubbers. Dibs had not worn his boots today. He shook his finger at me.

"Take off my rubbers," he said.

"You think *I* should take off my rubbers?" I asked him.

"Yes. Always. Indoors," he answered.

I reached down and removed my rubbers and put them in the corner. "How is that?" I asked.

"Better," he replied.

He tried to put the nipple back on the bottle but could not. He brought it over to me. "I can't," he said. "Help me."

"All right, I'll help you," I said, and put the nipple on the bottle for him. He took the bottle, immediately removed the nipple, and emptied the water in the sink. He turned and held the empty bottle out for me to see.

"Empty bottle," he said.

"Yes. You emptied it."

Dibs stood by the sink, holding the empty nursing bottle clasped closely to him, looking steadily at me for a long time. I looked at him, waiting for him to lead the way in either activity or conversation. Or to stand there and look and think, if he decided to do that.

"I am thinking," he said.

"You are?" I replied.

"Yes. I am thinking."

I did not press him to tell me what he was thinking. I wanted him to experience more than a question-and-answer exercise. I wanted him to feel and experience his total self in our relationship—and not to confine it to any one kind of behavior. I wanted him to learn that he was a person of many parts, with his ups and downs, his loves and hates, his fears and courage, his infantile desires and his more mature interests. I wanted him to learn by experience the responsibility of assuming the initiative to use his capacities in his relationships with people. I did not want to direct it into any single channel by praise, suggestion, questions. I might miss completely the essence of this child's total personality if I jumped to any premature conclusions. I waited while Dibs stood there thinking. A very slight and fleeting smile crossed his face.

"I will finger paint, play in the sand, and have a tea party," he said.

"You are planning what you want to do during the rest of our hour?" I asked.

"That's right," he replied. He smiled more openly now. "Quite often you are right," he added.

"Well, that's encouraging," I said.

He laughed. It was brief, but it was the first laugh I had heard from him. He took the tea set from the shelf. "I will get everything ready," he announced.

"Are you going to have the tea party first?" I asked.

"Yes. I think I will," he replied. He filled the nursing bottle with water, chewed the nipple which he did not put on the bottle, turned the water on full force, and closed the doors that shut the sink off in a closet. He looked at me, obviously waiting for my reaction to this. I said nothing. He walked across the room and leaned his elbow on the windowsill, holding the bottle in one hand, chewing on the nipple, looking steadily at me. Then he laughed, ran across the room to the closed-off sink, opened the doors, turned off the water. He emptied the nursing bottle, refilled it. He chewed and sucked the nipple. Then he opened one of the cupboard doors and looked up on the shelves where the supplies were stored. He looked at me.

"I'll take my leggings off now," he said, pointing to his snowpants, which he had worn for the first time today and had not removed.

"Think maybe you'll take them off, do you?" I asked.

"That's right," Dibs said. But instead of following through, he looked in the cupboard again and started to examine all the things on the shelf. He got out the boxes of clay. I explained to him that there was clay in the jar on the table and that the clay in the box was to be opened and used after the other was gone. I said the supplies were stored there to be used as needed.

"Oh, I see," Dibs said. "This is your supply closet."

"Yes," I replied.

He plucked at his snow pants. "My leggings," he said.

"What about your leggings?" I asked.

"There is a very cold wind outside today," he said.

"Yes. It is cold outside," I agreed.

"It is cold in the playroom today," Dibs said.

"Yes, it is," I replied.

"Then take off my leggings?" Dibs asked me.

"That is up to you," I said. "If you want to take them off, you may. If you don't want to today, that is all right, too, because it is cold in here today."

"That's right," Dibs answered. "Very, very cold."

The chimes struck four, but he seemed not to notice. He went over to the sand and climbed into the sandbox. He played with the airplanes and soldiers. He sighed.

"Take off your boots every place indoors," he said. "Pull and push and tug and get them off. It is hard to do. But leave your leggings on today, because it is cold in here."

"It seems as though there are some things we should

always take off whenever we are inside and some things we may sometimes leave on," I commented.

"That's right," Dibs said. "Mixes people up."

"It is sort of confusing," I remarked.

"It is very confusing," Dibs repeated. He nodded his head emphatically.

There was a very small one-room doll house in the sand-box. It had a broken shutter on one of the windows. Dibs repaired this, silently and efficiently. He got out the box of heavy cardboard farm animals with wooden stands. "Miss A will help you fix them, Dibs," he said. He turned to me and asked, "Will you help me fix them, Miss A?"

"What do you think?" I asked.

"You will help," he replied. He went ahead and inserted the animals in the stands without assistance. He started to sing as he worked. He placed the little house in the middle of the sandbox and set the farm animals around in different places. He seemed to be completely absorbed in his activity. "Cats live in this house," he said. "The fighting man has a cat, a real cat. And here is the duck. The duck has no pond and the duck wants a pond. You watch. Two ducks, there are. Here is the big duck and it is brave. Here is the little duck, but not so brave. The big duck may have a nice safe pond someplace. But this little duck does not have a pond of its own and it does want its own pond. But now these two ducks have met and they are standing here together and they are both watching the truck drive up outside the window."

His language was flowing out smoothly and effectively. I listened. I noted that as he had been speaking a big truck had driven up and parked outside the window of the playroom.

"So the little duck wants a safe pond of its own, perhaps like the one he thinks the big duck has?" I queried.

"That's right," Dibs said. "Together, they watch the big truck drive up. The truck parks, the man goes inside the building, he loads up his truck, and when it is filled it drives away."

"I see," I replied. Dibs took the toy truck and played out what he had told me. He was silent for a long time.

"Five more minutes, Dibs," I said. Dibs ignored my remark.

"I said there are five more minutes," I repeated.

"Yes," Dibs said, wearily. "I heard you."

"You heard me say five more minutes, but you didn't indicate that you did?" I asked.

"That's right," Dibs said. "Then I did."

"Yes. When I repeated it you did," I remarked. I was trying to taper off the hour so it would not end abruptly and without warning.

"This will all happen in five more minutes," Dibs said. He made a road through the sand, leading up to and around the house. "It makes a funny noise as it goes through the sand," he said. He looked at me and laughed. "The truck is full. As it goes it makes a track, a one-way track, and it dumps out the sand here." He quickly sorted through the soldiers, selected three, and put them in the truck. He covered them with sand. "This is a one-way road and these three people get in this truck and they don't ever come back."

"They go away and stay away?" I commented.

"That's right," Dibs said. "Forever." He pushed the truck through the sand, down under the sand, scooped sand up and buried the truck and the three figures. He sat there staring at the mound of sand and this made.

"Look, Dibs," I said. "This many more minutes," I held up three fingers.

He glanced at me. "Three more minutes," he said. He added more sand to the top of the pile, burying the truck and the unspecified people.

"Now, little duck," he said, gently. "You saw it happen. They are gone." Then he took the figure of the little duck and placed it on top of the hill he had made with the sand over the buried truck. He brushed the sand off his hands. He climbed out of the sandbox.

"Today is Valentine's Day," he said suddenly.

"Yes, it is," I replied.

"Leave them here all night and all day," he said. "Don't take them down."

"You want them to stay the way you have left them?" I remarked.

"That's right," Dibs said. He came up to me and touched the small note pad I had on my knee. "Write this down in your notes," he said. "Dibs came. He found the sand interesting today. Dibs played with the house and the fighting men for the last time. Goodbye!"

He picked up his coat and hat and walked out of the playroom, down the hall, into the reception room. His mother helped him on with his coat and hat. He left without another word.

I went into my office and sat down at the desk. What a child! One could speculate and interpret and probably be fairly accurate in concluding the significance of his symbolic play. However, it seemed to me that it would be unnecessary, redundant, and, perhaps, even restrictive, to have verbalized interpretation at this point—or to have attempted to probe for further information.

In my opinion, the therapeutic value of this kind of psychotherapy is based upon the child's experiencing himself as a capable, responsible person in a relationship that tries to communicate to him two basic truths: that no one ever really knows as much about any human being's inner world as does the individual himself; and that responsible freedom grows and develops from inside the person. The child must first learn self-respect and a sense of dignity that grows out of his increasing self-understanding before he can learn to respect the personalities and rights and differences of others.

Chapter Seven

THE FOLLOWING THURSDAY AFTERNOON when Dibs arrived at the Child Guidance Center, he greeted me with a quick smile, and walked back to the playroom ahead of me. He entered the playroom, went over to the doll house.

"This is different," he said. "Things have been changed."

"Someone else has probably been playing with them," I said.

"Yes," Dibs remarked. He whirled around and inspected the sandbox. "And the animals, too," he said. "They are not the way I left them."

Probably someone has been playing with them, too," I commented.

"That's the way it looks," Dibs said. He stopped in the middle of the room, listening. "Hear the typewriter?" he asked me. "Someone is working on a typewriter. Writing letters on a typewriter."

"Yes. I hear it," I replied.

Dibs had a knack of introducing safe, inanimate objects as subjects for his conversations that he seemed to use as a defensive shield when something bothered him. He was upset because the toys were not as he had left them. He had asked that they not be moved when he left the last time, but no promises and no explanations had been given him. This was purposely avoided because it seemed important for Dibs, as all children, to learn by experience that no part of his world is static and controllable. Now that he had encountered concrete evidence of his changing world it would be important to work with his reactions to it—not with reassurance, not with lengthy explanations or apologies, not with words, words, thrown at him as a substitute, but with the experience he might now have to take a measure of his own ability to cope with a changing world.

He walked over to the sandbox and stared into the flattened sand and the mixed figures lying around in it.

"Where's my little duck?" he asked.

You are wondering what happened to the little duck that you left on the top of the mound of sand?" I asked.

He turned quickly and looked directly at me. "That's right," he said, angrily. "Where is my little duck?"

"You said you wanted it left there and someone has moved it," I replied, trying to recapitulate the situation, slowing down his reactions by my responses so that he could more accurately identify his thoughts and feelings.

He walked up close to me and looked me straight in the eye. "That's right," he said, emphatically. "Why?"

"You wonder why I didn't see to it that they remained in the same places where you had left them," I commented.

"Yes," he said. "Why?"

"Why do you think I let that happen?" I asked him.

"I don't know," he said. "It makes me angry. You should have done it!"

Now it was my turn to ask the questions. "Why should I have done it?" I asked. "Did I promise you that I would?"

He looked down at the floor. "No," he replied, his voice dropping almost to a whisper.

"But you wanted me to do it?"

"Yes," he whispered. "I wanted you to do it just for me."

"Other children come in here and play with these things," I said. "Some one of them probably moved your duck."

"And my mountain," he said. "My little duck was standing on the top of my mountain."

"I know," I said. "And now your sand mountain is not in there, either, is it?"

"It is gone," he said.

"And you feel angry and disappointed because of it, don't you?" I asked.

Dibs nodded in agreement. He looked at me. I looked at him. What would ultimately help Dibs the most was not the sand mountain, not the powerful, little plastic duck, but the feeling of security and adequacy that they symbolized in the creation he had built last week. Now, faced with the disappearance of the concrete symbols, I hoped that he could experience within himself confidence and adequacy as he coped now with his disappointment and with the realization that things outside ourselves change— and many times we have little control over those elements, but if we learn to utilize our inner resources, we carry our security around with us.

He sat on the edge of the sandbox, silently looking at the scattered figures. Then he began to pick out some of the figures and separate them into similar types. He reached up and took my pencil. With this he tried to probe into a hole in one of the animal stands which was bent. He broke the point of the pencil.

"Oh, look," he said, casually. "The point broke." He handed the pencil to me. Now why had he done this?

I took the pencil. "I will go out and sharpen the pencil, Dibs," I said. "I'll be back in just a minute. You stay here," I left him.

This playroom, which we used so often as a part of our research into child behavior and for our professional training program, had, along one side, what seemed to be a large mirror. It was, in reality, a one-way vision glass. To anyone in the playroom, it served as a mirror. Behind it, in a darkened room, sat one or more carefully selected and specially trained observers who monitored the tape recorders and who also kept records of timed descriptions of behavior. Later the recordings were transcribed and edited to include the observed behavior of both child and therapist, with the time noted in minute intervals down the side of the reports. This we used for research data, for discussion in our advanced doctoral seminars as a part of the professional training program. All names and identifying information were changed before any of this material was used, so no one could ever identify any individuals involved. In our work, there is so much basic similarity in the psychological problems of the individuals involved that, even though one might feel what remains is identifying, in reality, with children's play, it cannot be.

When I left the room to sharpen my pencil, the observers behind the mirror continued their records.

Dibs picked up the shovel and dug in the sand. He talked to himself as he did. "All right, sand," he said. "Think you can stay here now and not be disturbed? And all you animals and people? I'll show you a thing or two. I'll dig you up. I'll find you. I'll find that man I buried. I'll dig and dig until I do." He dug quickly into the sand. Finally, he pulled out one of the soldiers. "So here you are," he said. "I'll get you now, you fighting man. Standing there so stiff and straight. Like an old iron railing from a fence, you are. I'll put you here, head down. I'll gouge you down into the sand."

He gouged the soldier, head down, into the sand until it was once again out of sight, buried. He brushed his hands together, rubbing off the sand. He smiled. He laughed. Then the expression in his voice changed to a gay and lifting tone and he said, "Take your hat and coat off, Dibs. It's cold in here."

I returned with my sharpened pencil. Dibs looked at me.

"It's cold in here," he said. "Take off my coat?"

"Well, it is cold in here," I replied. "Perhaps you had better leave your jacket on today."

"Turn the heat on," said Dibs. He went over to the radiator and touched it.

"The radiator is cold," he said.

"Yes, I know it is."

"I'll turn it on," Dibs announced. He turned on the radiator.

"Do you think that might make it warm in here?" I asked.

"Yes. If there is a fire in the basement," he said.

"A fire in the basement?" I asked.

"In the *furnace*," he replied. "In the furnace which is *in* the basement."

"Oh," I said. "Well, the furnace is out of order today. The men are down there fixing it."

"What is wrong with it?" Dibs asked.

"I don't know," I replied.

"You could find out, you know," he said, after a short interval.

"I could? How?"

"You could go down in the basement and hang around out of the way on the edge of things close enough to watch them and hear what they have to say," he told me.

"I expect I could," I replied.

"Then why didn't you?" he asked.

"To tell you the truth, Dibs," I replied, "It had not occurred to me to do that."

"You can learn lots of interesting things that way," he said.

"I'm sure of that," I told him. And I was just as sure that Dibs had learned many, many things in that manner, hanging around, out of the way, on the edge of things, close enough to watch people and hear what they had to say.

He walked over to the cupboards and looked in. "These are all empty," he said.

"That's right," I said. Now he had me checking off his observations!

"It's too cold to take off my leggings again, today," he said.

"I think so."

"The furnace must have been in the first part of its breakdown last Thursday," he said.

"That could be true," I agreed.

"But why else, if not that?" he asked. "Why else?"

"I don't know. I've never studied furnace breakdowns. I don't know much about them," I said.

Dibs laughed. "You only notice when it is cold," he said.

"That's right," I agreed. "I take it for granted that as long as it heats properly, it must be all right. When it doesn't, it must be in need of repair."

"Yes," he said, "then you notice it's broken."

"Then I notice," I agreed.

He wandered over to the table and picked up the nursing bottle and drank from it. He talked to me between sucks. "Miss A has no rubbers on today," he commented.

"No. I don't have them on in here today."

"That's good," he said. He dragged a chair over to the three-cornered closet in one corner of the room. A large square had been cut in this door and curtained. This made a puppet theater. He climbed up on the chair and, parting the curtains, looked inside. "Empty," he said.

He dragged the chair over to the sink, climbed up and looked into the cupboards over the sink. "Empty," he announced.

"There isn't anything up in those high cupboards," I said. But he checked them all. Then he pulled the chair out of the way, opened the doors that closed off the sink, turned on the water. He removed the nipple from the nursing bottle, while the water ran full force. He filled the bottle, poured the water in the sink, kept the nipple. He laid the nipple down on the table, turned off the water, picked up the gun, filled the gun with sand. He pulled the trigger and tried to shoot out the sand, but could not. The sand trickled out of the gun and fell on the floor. He sat down on the ledge around the sandbox, filled the gun again, pulled the trigger.

"It doesn't work this way," he said.

"I notice," I replied.

He brushed the sand back off the ledge into the sandbox. He was sitting facing me. He started to pick up the scattered animals, talking as he did so. "The rooster crows, cock-a-doodle-do," he said. "The rooster crows while the hen lays eggs. And the two ducks are in swimming. Oh, see! They have got *their* pond, their own little pond. The little duck says 'quack-quack' and the big duck says 'quack-quack.' And they swim around together in their safe little pond. And there are two rabbits. Two dogs. Two cows. Two horses. Two cats. There are two of everything. There is *nothing here alone!*"

He reached over and got the empty box in which the soldiers were usually kept. "This is the box for all the fighting men," he said. "It has a lid that can be kept on, oh, so tight."

He got on his knees on the ledge around the sandbox to examine the little house. He turned it around. "No *people* live in this house," he said. "Just the cat and the rabbit. Just one cat and one rabbit. Marshmallow is our rabbit's name at school," he added, glancing at me. "We keep it in a big cage in the corner of one of our rooms and sometimes we let it out to hop and jump around and sit and think."

"The cat and rabbit live in this house together?" I said. "And Marshmallow is the rabbit's name."

"The *school* rabbit's name," Dibs interrupted to say. "Not this rabbit that lives in the house with the cat. But we have a rabbit at school and that is the rabbit named Marshmallow. He is a very large, white rabbit—something like this one—this toy one. That is what reminded me of our school rabbit."

"Oh, I see. The pet rabbit is at school," I said.

"The *caged* rabbit," Dibs corrected. "But sometimes we let it out. And sometimes, when nobody is looking, *I* let it out."

This was the first reference Dibs had made to school. I wondered how he was getting along now. Was his behavior there the same now as it was the day I visited? When Dibs' mother had agreed to try the play sessions I had notified the school. I told the headmistress I would see Dibs if and when his mother brought him to the Center. I had said quite honestly that I did not know how he would respond to these play sessions—whether or not they would be helpful. We left it that the school would call me if and when they wanted another conference, or if they had any

observations, reports, or problems that we might discuss. I
did this because I felt it would be a little more objective to
receive unsolicited reports about his behavior, rather than
to get their response to my inquiries since I would be
personally involved in his therapy. I had not notified the
school that his mother had brought him in. The child's
parents are the ones to discuss his therapy appointments,
in my opinion. And no reports are given out to any person
or agency without the written consent and knowledge of
the parents.

I was interested in the remark Dibs had made about the
rabbit at school. This indicated that Dibs, even though not
an active, participating member of the group, was observing, learning, thinking, drawing conclusions as he crawled
around on the edge of things. It would be interesting to
know what he was doing in school and at home. It would
probably be interesting for the others who knew Dibs to
know what he was doing in the playroom. However, it
would not change the procedures I was using, because I
was concerned more with Dibs' present perception of his
world, his relationships, his feelings, his developing concepts, his conclusions, deductions, and inferences. I could
visualize Dibs letting the caged rabbit out for its freedom.
I could sense the affect that prompted that action.

He erected the cardboard fence around the animals.
"I'll make a door in the fence," he announced, cutting the
fence, bending back part of it to make an open gate.
"That's so the animals can always get out, whenever they
want to."

"I see," I commented.

He picked up the various odd-shaped bits of cardboard
that had been punched out to define the fence. He examined them carefully, critically. "This is .... This is ...."
He was trying to define the object. "Well," he announced.
"This is a piece of nothing. This is what nothing looks
like." He held it up for me to see. This was an interesting
inference—and accurate to a certain degree.

He picked out some of the toy soldiers. "This man here
has a gun," he said. "This one rides a horse. Here are

more fighting men." He lined them up on the outer ledge of the sandbox. "These, I will put into the box." He did. "And the truck is once again making a track around the house. The rabbit and the cat are looking out the window —just looking and watching."

He sat there, clasped his hands together in his lap, and looked at me for several minutes in silence. The expression on his face was serious, but his eyes were sparkling with his thoughts. He leaned toward me and spoke. "This isn't Independence Day," he said. "And it won't be until July fourth. But it comes on Thursday. It's four months and two weeks away and it comes on Thursday and I'll come and see Miss A. I looked on the calendar to see. Monday is July first. Tuesday is July second. Wednesday is July third. Wednesday is almost Independence Day, but not quite. Then comes July fourth which is Independence Day, and on Thursday I come here!" He reached over and picked up the toy rabbit. "Wednesday, July third, will be a long day—the morning, the afternoon, the nighttime. And then comes the next morning's light. Independence Day, Fourth of July, Thursday, and *I will be here!*"

"You must really like to come here," I said.

"Oh, I do!" Dibs replied. "I do!" He smiled. Then he sobered quickly and continued speaking. "Independence Day is the soldiers' and the sailors' day. The drums go boom, boom, boom. And the flags are out." He sang a marching song. He dug in the sand. He filled the truck with the sand. He pushed it around. "It is a gay day," he said. "Independence Day! And they are all staggered by their joy. These soldiers are unloading freedom and unlocking all the doors!"

The beauty and power of this child's language was impressive. And to think that it had grown and flourished, even though it had been driven undercover into the wilderness of his anxiety by his loneliness and fear. But now he had waded into his fear and was growing strong with the certainties he discovered. He was exchanging his anger and fear and anxiety for hope and confidence and gladness. His sadness and sense of defeat were thawing out.

"You, too, feel that gladness, don't you, Dibs?" I said, after a while.

"It is a joy I would not want to lose," he replied. "I come with gladness into this room."

I looked at him, sitting on the ledge of the sandbox, radiating the sense of peace he was feeling now. He looked so small, and yet so filled with hope and courage and confidence that I could feel the power of his dignity and assurance.

"I come with gladness into this room," he said again. "I leave it with sadness."

"You do? And does any of the gladness go out with you?" I asked.

Dibs buried three toy soldiers in the sand. "This makes *them* unhappy," he said. "They cannot see. They cannot hear. They cannot breathe," he explained. "Dibs, dig them out of there," he ordered himself. "First thing you know, it'll be time to go. Do you want to leave them buried, Dibs?" he asked himself.

In five more minutes it will be time to go," I said. "Well, do you want to leave them buried?"

He jumped quickly out of the sandbox. "I'll play with the fighting men here on the floor," he said. "I'll line them up in order." He flopped down on the floor and arranged the soldiers. He reached into the sandbox and dug out the soldiers he had buried. He looked at them carefully. He held one out toward me. "This is Papa," he said, identifying it.

"Oh? That one is Papa, is it?" I remarked, casually.

"Yes," he replied. He stood it on the floor in front of him, shut his fist, knocked it over, stood it up, knocked it over with his fist. He repeated this several times. Then he looked at me. "Four more minutes left?" he asked.

"That's right," I said, glancing at my *watch*. "Four more minutes left."

"Then it'll be time to go home," Dibs said.

"Umhmm," I said.

He played with the "Papa" soldier, again, standing it up, knocking it down. Again he looked at me. "Three more minutes left." he asked.

"That's right," I said. I added, "Then it'll be time to go home." I said this more to determine what he might reply than to call his attention to a fact he already knew.

"That's right," Dibs replied. "Even if I don't want to go home, it will be time to go home."

"Yes, Dibs," I replied. "Even if you don't want to go home, it will be time to go."

"That's right," Dibs said. He sighed. He sat there in silence for another minute. He seemed to have an uncanny sense of time. "Two more minutes?" he asked.

"Yes."

"I come back next Thursday," he stated.

"Yes, you do," I agreed.

"Tomorrow is Washington's Birthday," he said. "That's Friday. Saturday is nothing. Sunday is the twenty-fourth. Then comes Monday and I go back to school!" he announced. There was a bright, happy gleam in his eyes.

Even though Dibs' outward behavior at school might not indicate it, school meant much to him. Even though his teachers might be baffled, frustrated, and feel a sense of defeat, they had gotten through to Dibs. He knew what was going on there. That marching song was probably one the children had been taught at school. Marshmallow was their pet—rather, their caged animal. But Marshmallow was a part of the school experience. I thought of that school conference. I recalled Miss Jane's recital of her monologue on the principles of magnetic attraction. The teachers should take heart. We never know how much of what we present to children is accepted by them, each in his own way, and becomes some part of the experiences with which they learn to cope with their worlds.

"We get the Elementary School News on Monday," Dibs said. "There will be a bright yellow, blue, and white cover on this one. And thirteen pages. There is a sign on the bulletin board in the hall that tells us. And then there is Tuesday and Wednesday and Thursday. And on Thursday, I'll be here, again!"

"You've got a pretty good idea of what this next week holds, haven't you? Washington's Birthday, the school newspaper, all the days in the week, then back here again," I commented.

"Yes," said Dibs.

And you can really read far beyond your years, I thought. And comprehend what you read. But I made no comment about his reading. He was taking it for granted; so would I. Even though he obviously was an excellent reader, that was not sufficient unto itself for the effectiveness of his total development.

"One more minute?" he asked.

"Yes. One more minute," I replied.

He picked up the figure he had identified as "Papa" and tossed it into the sandbox. "Papa is picking me up here, today," Dibs told me.

"Oh?" I exclaimed, pricking up my ears. So "Papa" was emerging a little into Dibs' world!

"Yes," Dibs said. He looked at me. I looked at him. The time was up and we both knew it, but neither of us said a word about it. Finally, Dibs stood up. "Time is up," he said, with a deep sigh.

"Yes, it is," I agreed.

"I wanta paint," Dibs said.

"You mean you don't want to leave, even though you know the time is up," I said.

Dibs glanced at me. There was a flicker of a smile on his face. He reached down and quickly moved each toy soldier that he had stood on the floor. He lined them up, aiming at me. He walked toward the door. "Guns are useful when it comes to shooting," he said.

"So I see," I replied.

He picked up his cap and walked down the hall. I walked down with him. I wanted to see "Papa."

"Goodbye," Dibs said, dismissing me.

"Goodbye, Dibs. I'll see you next Thursday."

"Papa" glanced at me. "How do you do," he said, stiffly. He seemed very ill at ease.

"How do you do," I replied.

"I say, Papa," Dibs said. "Do you know today is not Independence Day?"

"Come, Dibs. I am in a hurry," "Papa" said.

"And it won't be until July," Dibs persisted. "But it comes on a Thursday, four months, two weeks away."

"Come, Dibs," "Papa" said, embarrassed to death by Dibs' conversation that probably seemed very bizarre to him—if, indeed, he was listening to it.

"Independence Day comes on Thursday," Dibs tried again. "On the Fourth of July is the day."

"Papa" was shoving Dibs out the door. "Can't you stop that senseless jabber?" he said, between clenched teeth.

Dibs sighed. He drooped. He left, silently, with his father.

The receptionist looked at me. There were no other people in the waiting room. "The old goat!" she said. "Why doesn't he go jump in the East River?"

"Yes," I agreed. "Why doesn't he?"

I went back to the playroom to straighten it up for the next young client. The observers came in to help. One of them told me what Dibs had said when I went out to sharpen my pencil. The tape had been rewound, and we listened as that part of the recording was played back. "What a kid!" one of the observers said.

And how perceptive, I thought. "Standing there so stiff and straight. Like an old iron railing from a fence, you are!" That's what Dibs had said. I felt like leaving "Papa" buried there in the sand for a week, myself. He had not been listening to the child. Dibs tried to converse with him, but he dismissed it as senseless jabbering. Dibs must have tremendous inner strength to have maintained a personality as effective as his in the face of such attacks upon it.

Sometimes it is very difficult to keep firmly in mind the fact that the parents, too, have reasons for what they do——have reasons, locked in the depths of their personali-ties, for their inability to love, to understand, to give of themselves to their children.

Chapter Eight

THE NEXT MORNING I received a telephone call from Dibs' mother. She asked if it would be convenient to arrange for an appointment for herself. She seemed to be apologetic about making this request, quickly adding that she would understand if I was too busy. I looked at my calendar and suggested several possible times, one for that morning, for that afternoon, for Monday, Tuesday, Wednesday afternoons. She had a wide range of times from which to choose. She hesitated, asked which time I preferred, suggested that I name the time. I told her that it made no difference to me; whatever appointment would be most convenient for her would be satisfactory as far as I was concerned. I told her that I would be at the Center at all the times I had mentioned so she could feel free to name the time that she preferred. Again she hesitated. Then, after considerable thought, she made her decision. "I will be there this morning at ten," she said. "Thank you. I do appreciate this."

I wondered what had prompted her decision to ask for a conference. Was she pleased, dissatisfied, or upset about Dibs? Had her husband reacted unfavorably to his brief visit to the Center the day before when he had called for Dibs? She would be at the Center in less than an hour. Perhaps, then, we would find out a little more about the situation.

It was difficult to predict how such a conference would develop. The mother might freeze up and be no more able to delve into the problem than she had been before. Then, again, she might be so full of unhappiness, frustration,

82

and a sense of personal inadequacy and defeat that she would welcome the opportunity to share at least a part of it with someone else. It would be extremely important to try to keep to a minimum any threat to her, and to attempt to communicate to her a feeling of confidential security in this conference. One thing I could be very sure of, this would be an extremely difficult and emotionally exhausting conference for this mother, no matter how she used the time—whether she was silent, or talked about safe but irrelevant things, or asked questions, or told a bit of her own closely guarded story. It would be my responsibility to communicate to her as effectively as I could, primarily by my attitude and personal philosophy, that her private, personal world belonged to her and she would be the one to decide if she wanted to unlock the door and share any part of it with me. And if she did so decide, I would not rush past her psychologically, and try to drag out anything that she did not offer voluntarily and with confidence in her ability to share her inner world with another person. And if she did not choose to open that door, I most certainly had no intention of even knocking on it, let alone attempting to force it open by intentional probing. It would be interesting to hear what she could tell about Dibs and about herself, but far more important to give her the experience of being a person of dignity, respected and acknowledged as an individual who has absolute ownership of her own deeply personal life.

She arrived promptly at the Center. We went back to my office immediately. She had previously made it clear that she felt extremely uncomfortable waiting in the reception room. And since she kept her appointment so promptly it seemed important to see her when she arrived and not require her to wait when it was not necessary.

She sat down in the chair beside my desk, facing me. She was very pale. Her hands were clasped tightly together. Her eyes flitted around, glancing at me and away quickly—as Dibs had done when I first saw him in the playroom.

I offered her a cigarette.

"No, thank you," she said.

I left the package on the desk. She motioned to it.

"I don't smoke," she said. "But if you want to, please do."

"I don't smoke, either," I replied. I put the package of cigarettes back in the desk drawer, more to break the strain of the first few minutes, than for any other purpose. I took my time doing it, then I looked at her. She had an expression of anxiety and panic in her eyes. It was important not to push her into any discussion of her problems, important not to assume the leadership by asking questions, important not to convert this session into a discussion of trivialities. If *she* wanted to do any of those things, that would be entirely different; for me to do it would be to defeat the purpose of the interview. She had asked for the conference. She had a reason for so doing. If I had asked her to come in for the appointment, it would have been my responsibility to get the interview underway.

This is the most difficult and crucial time of any initial interview and it determines greatly the effectiveness of the total experience. To attempt to explain the purpose of such a conference is also fruitless so many times that I would not bother to interject any explanation—or any "structuring of the experience," as it is sometimes called. The silence did not make me feel ill at ease. I was confident that she could cope with it far more constructively than any effort I might make for the sake of starting a conversation. We did not want a conversation for the sake of a conversation.

"I don't know where to begin," she said.

"I know. Sometimes it is difficult to get started," I said. She smiled, but it was a smile without mirth. "So much to say," she said. "And so much to say!"

"That's quite often the case," I said.

"Some things are better left unsaid," she told me, looking directly at me.

"At times, it seems so," I replied.

"But so many unsaid things can become a great burden," she said.

"Yes. That can happen, too," I commented.

She sat there looking out the window in silence for a long time. She was beginning to relax. "You have a very lovely view out this window," she remarked. "That church out there is beautiful. It looks so big and strong and peaceful."

"Yes, it does," I said.

She looked down at her tightly folded hands. She looked up and met my eyes. There were tears in her eyes. "I am so worried about Dibs," she said. "So deeply worried about him."

This comment I had not anticipated. I tried to accept her remark as casually as possible. "Worried about him?" I asked. No more than that at this point. I did not ask her why.

"Yes," she said. "So very worried! Lately, he seems to be so unhappy. He stands around, looking at me, always so silent. He comes out of his room more often now. But he just stands around on the edge of things, like a haunting shadow. And whenever I speak to him, he runs away. Only to return and regard me with such tragic sorrow in his eyes." She took some tissues from the box on the desk and wiped her eyes.

This was indeed an interesting observation. Dibs was coming out of his room more often, now. And according to her report, *lately*, he seemed to be *more unhappy*. Of course, it could be that she was more aware of his unhappiness than she had been previously. It could be that Dibs was showing his feelings more overtly at home. And to maintain silence, when he had such a command of language, indicated that he had tremendous inner strength and control.

"I feel very uncomfortable when he does that," she added, after a long pause. "It is as though he is asking for something—something that I cannot give. He is a very difficult child to understand. I have tried. Really, I have tried. But I have failed. From the beginning, when he was an infant, I could not understand him. I had never really known any children before Dibs. I had no real experience

as a woman with children or babies. I didn't have the
slightest idea what they were like, really like as persons,
that is. I knew all about them biologically, physically, and
medically. But I could never understand Dibs. He was
such a heartache—such a disappointment from the moment of his birth. We hadn't planned on having a child.
His conception was an accident. He upset all our plans. I
had my professional career, too. My husband was proud
of my accomplishments. My husband and I were very
happy before Dibs was born. And when he was born he
was so different. So big and ugly. Such a big, shapeless
chunk of a thing! Not responsive at all. In fact, he rejected
me from the moment he was born. He would stiffen and
cry every time I picked him up!" Tears were streaming
down her face and she wiped them off with the tissues as
she talked, almost sobbing out her story. I began to speak,
but she silenced me.

"Please, don't say anything," she pleaded. "I've got to
get it out, at least this one time. I've carried this around
with me for too long. It is like a heavy stone in the middle
of my heart. Think whatever you will about me, but,
please, let me tell you. I didn't intend to do this. When I
called and asked for the appointment, I intended to ask
you about Dibs. His father was upset yesterday. He thinks
the therapy is making Dibs worse. But there is something that I just must talk to you about. I've kept it all
locked up inside of me for so long a time.

"My pregnancy was very difficult. I was very ill most of
the time. And my husband resented my pregnancy. He
thought that I could have prevented it. Oh, I don't blame
him. I resented it, too. We couldn't do any of the things
we used to do together, couldn't go anyplace. I suppose I
should say that we didn't, not couldn't. My husband
stayed away more and more, buried himself in his work.
He is a scientist, you know. A brilliant man! But remote.
And very, very sensitive. And this may surprise you. I
don't even talk about this anymore. I've never even mentioned it at the school." Again, there was that unhappy,
mirthless smile on her lips.

"Before I became pregnant, I was a surgeon. I loved my work. And I had shown promise of achieving success as a surgeon. I had perfected two very complicated heart operations. My husband was proud of me. All our friends were very brilliant, successful, interesting men and women. And then Dibs was born and spoiled all our plans and our life. I felt that I had failed miserably. I decided that I would give up my work. Some of my closest professional friends couldn't understand my attitude, or my decision. I did not tell them about Dibs. Oh, they knew about my pregnancy. But not about Dibs. It soon became obvious that Dibs was not normal. It was bad enough to have a child, but to have a mentally retarded child was really more than we could bear. We were ashamed. We were humiliated. There had never been anything like this in either of our families. My husband, noted throughout the country for his brilliance. And my own record had always been outstanding. All our values had been heavily slanted in the direction of intelligence—fine, precise, noteworthy intellectual achievement!

"And our families. We had both grown up in families where those qualities were valued above all others. And then Dibs! So peculiar. So remote. So untouchable. Not talking. Not playing. Slow to walk. Striking out at people like a little wild animal. We were so ashamed. We didn't want any of our friends to know about him. We cut ourselves off socially more and more from our friends, because if we continued to have them in, naturally they would want to see the baby. And we didn't want anyone to see him. We were so ashamed. And I had lost all confidence in myself. I could not go on with my work. I knew that I would not be able to perform an operation ever again!

"There was no place we could send him. We tried to solve the problem as best we could. We didn't want anyone to know about him. I took him to a neurologist, one out on the West Coast. I used another name. We didn't want anyone to know what we suspected. But the neurologist couldn't find anything organically wrong with Dibs.

Then, a little over a year ago we took him to a psychiatrist, again, not in this area. We thought that we would leave him in this particular home for a psychiatric and psychological diagnosis. I felt that Dibs was schizophrenic. Or autistic, if not mentally retarded. I felt that his symptoms suggested definite brain damage. The psychiatrist insisted on seeing my husband and me for several interviews. This was the only time we ever revealed our true identity to any physician whom we consulted about Dibs. It was a shocking experience. The psychiatrist interviewed us. They probed without mercy into our very personal and private lives. When we felt they were going far beyond any professional need in their questions, the social workers told us we were being hostile and resistive. They seemed to take a sadistic pleasure in their insensitive, cruel persecution.

"The the psychiatrist told us, that in view of our backgrounds, he would be very frank with us. He said that Dibs was not mentally defective or psychotic or brain-damaged, but the most rejected and emotionally deprived child he had ever seen. He said that my husband and I were the ones who needed the help. He suggested treatment for both of us. It was the most shocking experience we had either of us ever had. Anyone could see that my husband I had been functioning adequately. We had never been inclined to free and easy social life, but the few friends and professional colleagues we had respected us, and respected our desire to have our own private lives our own way! We had never had any personal problems that we could not cope with ourselves.

"We brought Dibs back home and got along as best we could. But it very nearly wrecked our marriage.

"We never mentioned the experience to anyone. Never told our families. Never told the school. But my husband stayed away more and more. Dorothy had been born a year after Dibs. I thought another child might help him. But they never got along. But Dorothy has always been a perfect child. Certainly she is proof that the fault is not ours. Then we sent Dibs to the private school where you first met him.

"I tell you no one knows the terrible tragedy and agony it is to have a mentally handicapped child! The only person he has ever related to has been his grandmother. She was with us the first month of his life—and visited us once a month for three years until she moved to Florida. After that she would come twice a year and stay for about a month each time she came. Dibs always remembered her, always made up to her when she came, always missed her desperately when she left. And he seemed to count the days until she would return.

"I have done everything I could for Dibs. We have given him everything money could buy, hoping that it would help. Toys. Music. Games. Books. His playroom is filled with everything we have thought might entertain, educate, and amuse him. And he has, at times, seemed to be happy in his room at home. He has always seemed happier alone. That's why we sent Dorothy away to a boarding school near here. She comes home on weekends and vacations. I think Dibs is happier with her out of the house. I think she is happier at the school. They do not get along at all well. Dibs strikes out at her like a wild animal if she goes near him or goes into his room.

"Lately, he seems so unhappy. And he seems to have changed. Then, yesterday, when my husband brought Dibs home, he was upset. They were both upset. He said that Dibs was babbling like an idiot. He said it in front of Dibs." She broke down and sobbed bitterly. "Then, I asked what Dibs had said and he said that Dibs was just babbling like an idiot! Dibs walked across the room, grabbed a chair and threw it over, knocked some things off the coffee table with a sweep of his hand, screamed at his father 'I hate you! I hate you!' ran up to him and kicked him again and again. My husband grabbed Dibs and after a struggle finally carried him up to his room and locked him in. When my husband came down I was crying. I couldn't help it. I know he doesn't like scenes. I know he despises tears. But I couldn't stand it. I said to him, 'Dibs wasn't babbling like an idiot now. He said he hated you!' Then, my husband sat down in a chair and actually wept! It was terrible. I had never seen a man cry before. I had never thought anything could cause my husband to shed a tear. I was afraid, suddenly terrified, because he seemed to be just as scared as I was. I think we were closer to each other then than we have ever been. Suddenly, we were just two frightened, lonely, unhappy people with our defenses crumpled and deserted. It was terrible—and yet a relief to know that we could be human, and could fail and admit that we had failed! Finally, we pulled ourselves together and he said that maybe we had been wrong about Dibs. I said I would come and ask you what you thought about Dibs." She looked at me with an expression of fear and panic in her eyes. "Tell me," she said. "Do you think that Dibs is mentally defective?"

"No," I replied, answering her question and saying no more than she asked to hear. "I do not think Dibs is mentally defective."

There was a long pause. She sighed deeply. "Do you . . . do you think he will be all right and that he will learn to act like other children?" she asked.

"I think so. But more important, I think that *you* will be able to answer that question yourself far more accurately than I can as you live with him at home, talk with him, play with him, observe him. I think you, probably, could tentatively answer it now," I said.

She nodded her head, slowly. "Yes," she said, and her voice had dropped almost to a whisper, "I have noticed many things about Dibs that indicate that he has some ability. But he seems so unhappy as he unfolds more and more at home. He doesn't have those awful temper tantrums any more. Not at home and not at school. That scene yesterday wasn't a tantrum. It was his protest at the insult he must have felt in his father's remark. He doesn't suck his thumb all the time any more. He is talking more and more at home. But to himself—not to us. Except for that outcry to his father. He is changing. He is improving, I only hope to God that he will be all right!" she said fervently.

"I hope so, too," I answered. There was a long silence.

Finally, she took her compact out of her handbag and powdered her face. "I can't remember when I have cried like this," she said. She pointed to the box of tissues. "You seem to be prepared, though; so, probably I'm not the only one who does cry on your shoulder."

"No. You have lots of company," I said.

She smiled. She and Dibs had so many little mannerisms in common. "I can't tell you how much I appreciate this," she said. "It doesn't seem possible an hour is up. But I hear the chimes. It is eleven o'clock."

I wouldn't have been too surprised if she had said at this point that she did not want to go home! "Time sometimes seems to get away from us in here," I said.

"Yes," She stood up, put on her coat. "Thank you for everything," she said; and she left.

No matter how many times we hear this kind of outpouring (and it happens frequently), the complexity of human motivation and behavior is demonstrated over and over again. There is no single isolated experience or feeling that triggers reaction patterns. There is always an accumulation of experiences intertwined with highly personal emotions, goals, values, that motivate the person and that determine his reaction. What had she said as a preface to her story? "So much to say. And so much not to say! Some things are better left unsaid. But so many unsaid things can become a burden."

She was aware of the elements that weighed so heavily upon her conscience. Probably more aware of the things she wanted to leave unspoken, made even more aware of them by the constant vigilance she maintained to guard their secrecy. Probably she and her husband had learned early in their lives that their keen intelligences could be erected as a shield around them, could insulate them from emotions that they had never learned to understand and use constructively.

Dibs had learned this, too. Read everything in sight,

display this skill when confronted by uncomfortable emotional reactions, dodge any head-on confrontation of a feeling. It was protective behavior.

His mother and father were still the victims of their lack of self-understanding and emotional maturity. They felt keenly their inability to relate affectively to Dibs. And probably with Dorothy. They were floundering around in the depths of their feelings of inadequacy and insecurity. When she asked me if I thought Dibs was mentally defective, I could have told her, with emphasis, that Dibs was indeed not mentally defective; more likely, he was a child of superior intelligence. And yet, to have made such an evaluation at this time might have defeated its best purpose. It could have intensified a feeling of guilt that had been indicated by the scene she had described between Dibs and his father and her reactions to it on the preceding day. And if Dibs' mother and father had accepted my evaluation, they might have concentrated on Dibs' intellectual endowment as a central point of his development. He had been utilizing quite fully his intelligence. It was the lack of balance in his total development that created the problem. Or, perhaps, quite unconsciously, they chose to see Dibs as a mental defective rather than as an intensified personification of their own emotional and social inadequacy. It was all speculation.

The crux of the problem was not an intellectual diagnosis of the reasons behind their behavior—although many people accept this tenet as basic to improved personal development. If you understand why you do and feel certain ways, many people believe, then you can change your ways. I've often thought, though, what with such understandings, the greatest changes are usually in the external behavior and gradually this brings about changes of motivation and feelings. I think it takes much longer to achieve this kind of change. And sometimes it seems to require an intense preoccupation with the self that puts the focus out of proportion to the place of an individual in his relationship with others—makes his world more self-centered, even though his external activities may try to belie this.

There are many different theoretical formulations of personality structure and therapy. This accounts for the different methods employed in psychotherapy, because method is the implementation of a basic theoretical formulation.

As for Dibs' mother, it seemed to me that it was highly unlikely that she could have been unaware of her child's intellectual endowment—at least to some degree. Out of her total experience, intellectual achievement alone had not been a very satisfactory answer. Her failure to relate to her child with love, respect, and understanding was probably due to her own emotional deprivation. Who can love, respect, understand another person, if they have not had such basic experiences themselves? It seemed to me that it would be more helpful for her to have learned in this interview that she was respected and understood, even though that understanding was, of necessity, a more generalized concept which accepted the fact that she had reasons for what she did, that she had capacity to change, that changes must come from within herself, that all changes—hers, her husband's, Dibs'—were motivated by many accumulative experiences. How had she phrased it? "Two frightened, lonely, unhappy people with their defenses crumpled and deserted . . . a relief to know that we could be human, and could fail and admit that we had failed."

Chapter Nine

DIBS CAME INTO THE PLAYROOM quite happily the following Thursday. His mother had called to ask if it would be
possible for Dibs to come fifteen minutes earlier because
she had to take him to the pediatrician for some shots.
This had been arranged.

When Dibs came into the playroom he said, "Today is
the day I see the doctor for a shot. The appointment has
been made."

"Yes, I know," I replied. "Well, you'll get there on
time."

"I'm glad about the change of time," he said, grinning
at me.

"You are," I replied. "Why?"

"I'm glad because I *feel* glad," he told me. That ended
that. He walked over to the doll house. "I see I have a job
to do," he said.

"What is that?"

"This," he answered, motioning to the doll house. "Fix
it up and lock it up. Lock the door! Close the windows."
He walked over to the window in the playroom and
looked out. He glanced back at me. "The sun shines," he
said. "It is very, very warm outside today. I'll take my
things off." He removed his hat, coat, leggings without any
help, walked over, hung them on the doorknob.

"I would like very much to paint today," he said.

"Well, that's up to you," I said.

"Yes," said Dibs. "It's up to me." He went over to the
easel. "I'll take off the lids and I'll put a brush in each
color. Now I'll put them in order. Red. Orange. Yellow.

94

Blue. Green," he said. He glanced back at me. "Some things are up to me. Others are not," he commented, briskly.

"Yes, I suppose that is true," I said.

"It *is* true," he replied, emphatically. He continued to rearrange the paints in the color sequence. Then he started to paint streaks of paint on his paper. "Whoops! Paint runs," he said. "Now crayons do not run," he added. "They stay where you put them. But paints? No. They run. I'll paint a blob of orange. See it run? Then a stripe of green. And down it drips. As it drips down, I'll wipe it off."

He reached over and tapped his fingers upon the mirrored wall. "That's someone else's room in there," he said. "Before, some people were sitting in that darkened room, but not today."

I was surprised at this unexpected announcement. "You think so, do you?" I asked.

"I *know* it," he said. "Little sounds and hushed voices have told me so."

This bit of evidence indicates how aware children are of the things around them, even though they may make no comment at the time—true of Dibs and of all children. True of us too. We do not comment verbally about everything we hear, see, think, infer. Probably only a very small percentage of our individual learning experiences are verbally communicated to others.

"Have you known it, too?" he asked me.

"Yes," I replied.

He turned back to the easel and painted more streaks of color on the paper. "These are streaks and stripes of my thoughts," he said.

"They are?"

"Yes. And now I will get out the fighting men. Especially that one particular fighting man."

As he crossed from the easel to the sandbox, he paused beside me and looked at my notes. I had abbreviated the names of the colors he had used by jotting down the first letter of each word. Dibs studied my notes, which were only records of actions, not his words. They were being recorded by the more silent observers monitoring the tape recorder.

"Oh, spell it out," Dibs said. "R is for red. R-E-D spells red. O is for orange. O-R-A-N-G-E. Y is for yellow. Y-E-L-L-O-W." And he spelled them all out in this fashion.

"Because you can spell all the names of the colors, do you think I should do it, too?" I asked him. "Don't you think I should abbreviate them, if I feel like abbreviating them?"

"Hmmm?" he said. "Well, yes. Don't do that to them. Always do things correctly. Spell them out. Do it right."

"Why?" I asked.

Dibs looked at me. He smiled. "Because I say so," he said.

"Is that reason enough?" I asked.

"Yes," Dibs said. "Unless you would rather do it your way." He laughed. He walked to the table, took a ball of clay out of the jar, tossed it in the air, caught it, replaced it in the jar. There was a small picture on the floor by the waste basket. He picked it up, looked at it. "Oh say," he remarked. "I do want this. I want to cut it out—these little figures here. Where are the scissors?"

I handed him a pair of scissors. He cut out the picture. Then he walked over to the doll house. "I have a job to do today," he announced.

"You have?"

"Yes." Very carefully, he removed all the walls from the doll house and carried them over to the sandbox. He took a shovel and dug a deep hole in the sand and buried the walls. Then he went back to the doll house and with a sturdy metal shovel pried the door off the doll house, and buried it in the sand. He worked quickly, efficiently, silently, intently. When he had completed this task, he looked at me. "I got rid of all the walls. And the door," he said.

"Yes, I see you did."

He then took the front wall of the doll house that now

had a doorway, but no door, and tried to stand it up in the sand. Finally, he succeeded. He selected a little car and pushed it around in the sand. He was perched on the ledge of the sandbox, leaning over in what seemed an awkward, uncomfortable position. He surveyed the situation.

"I will have to get completely into the sandbox," he said. He crawled into the sandbox, sat down in the middle of it, looked at me, grinned. "Today, I got into the sand," he said. "Little by little, I got into the sand. A little way in time before last, and last time, and now this time."

"Yes, you did," I replied. "And now, today, you are all the way in."

"Sand is getting into my shoes," he observed. "So, I'll take off my shoes." He took off one shoe. He pushed his foot down under the sand. Then he turned over and lay face down in the sand, rubbed his cheeks against the sand, stuck out his tongue and tasted the sand. He gritted the sand between his teeth. He looked up at me.

"Why, this sand is gritty and sharp and it tastes like nothing," he said. "Is this what nothing tastes like?" He grabbed up a handful of sand and trickled it down on his head, rubbed the sand into his hair. He laughed. Suddenly, he stuck his foot up in the air. "Look," he shouted, "I gotta hole in my sock. I gotta holey sock on one foot!"

"So I see," I commented.

He stretched out full-length in the sandbox. He rolled over. He wiggled down in the sand, and with his hands scooped the sand on top of him. His movements were free, expansive, relaxed. "Hand me the nursing bottle," he commanded. I handed it to him. "I'll pretend this is my little crib," he said. "I'll curl up in a nice, cozy ball and play I'm a baby again." He did, sucking contentedly on the nursing bottle. Suddenly, he sat up, grinning at me.

"I shall sing it to you," he announced. "I will make up a song and sing it just for you. Okay?"

"Okay," I replied.

He sat there, cross-legged. "I am thinking," he said.

"Okay. You think, if you feel like it," I replied.

He laughed. "I will compose the words as I go along," he said.

"All right."

He took a deep breath. Then he started to sing. He seemed to be composing the music, too. His voice was clear, melodious, and sweet. The music presented a contrast to the words he composed. His hands were clasped together. His expression was serious. He looked like a little choir boy. The words, though, were not choir-boy words.

"Oh, I hate—hate—hate," he sang. "I hate the walls and the doors that lock and the people who shove you in. I hate the tears and the angry words and I'll kill them all with my little hatchet and hammer their bones and spit on them." He reached down in the sand, picked up a toy soldier, pounded it with the rubber hatchet, spit on it. "I spit in your face. I spit in your eye. I gouge your head down deep in the sand," he sang. His voice rang out, sweetly and clearly. "And the birds do fly from the east to the west and it is a bird that I want to be. Then I'll fly away over the walls, out the door, away, away, away from all my enemies. I'll fly and fly around the world and I'll come back to the sand, to the playroom, to my friend. I'll dig in the sand. I'll bury in the sand. I'll throw the sand. I'll play in the sand. I'll count all the grains of the sand and I'll be a baby again."

He sucked on the nursing bottle again. He grinned at me. "How did you like my song?" he asked.

"That was quite a song," I replied.

"Yes," he said. "Quite a song." He got out of the sandbox, walked over to me, looked at my watch. "Ten more minutes," he said, and held up ten fingers.

"Yes. Ten more minutes," I replied.

"*You* think it'll be ten more minutes and then it'll be time to go home," he said.

"That's right. That's what *I* think," I replied. "What do *you* think?"

"Aha!" he exclaimed. "You want to know? Well, I think, soon it'll be time to go. I'll get out the rest of the fighting men. These two are with guns. And this airplane. Like a bird. Airplane, fly. Oh, airplane, full of sand. Fly around. Fly around. Fly up to the sky!" He ran around the playroom, holding the airplane aloft, moving with grace and rhythm. "Oh airplane, tell me! How high can you fly? Can you fly up to the blue, blue sky? Can you fly beyond the sky? To the clouds and the winds that hold fast the rain up there so high? Can you fly? Tell me, lovely airplane, can you fly? Oh Oh airplane. . . ." Abruptly, he stopped all activity. He listened intently. He dropped the airplane down into the sand. Suddenly, all the exuberance and joy seemed to have been dashed out of him.

"There is Dorothy," he said. He went over to the sandbox, climbed in, and with his shovel dug out the door and the walls of the doll house. "These cannot be buried, yet," he said. He looked at me, distress tightening his lips, wrinkling his forehead. "Now nine more minutes?" he asked me, his voice flattened by his sadness.

"No. Only five more minutes left," I told him.

"Oh?" said Dibs, holding up five fingers. "Where did the other four go?"

"You didn't think that four minutes had gotten past you?"

"It'll soon be time to go home," Dibs said. "Even if I don't want to go home. Even so, it'll be the time will come that tells us this is at the end."

"Yes," I replied. "Even so, the time comes to a close."

There was the sound of the truck leaving. "There goes our truck," Dibs said. "Did you hear it?"

"I heard it."

"It is time for the truck to go home, too," Dibs said.

"Yes, I suppose it is."

"The truck may not want to go home, either," Dibs said.

"That is possible," I said.

"How many more minutes are there left?" Dibs asked.

"Three minutes."

Dibs held the door of the doll house in his hands and looked at it. "I'll have to put this back on the doll house and lock all the windows," he said. "Where is the hammer to nail on the door?"

"There isn't any in here, now," I said. "Put it on the shelf—or in the doll house, if you want to. The custodian will put it back on later."

Dibs laid it on the table, changed his mind, removed it and put it in the doll house. He closed the doll house windows.

"Help me with my shoe," he said, handing me his shoe, sitting down on a little chair while I put it on for him. "Help me with my hat and coat," he said, suddenly becoming very helpless. I did.

"The people are all in the house asleep," he said. "And it is an early spring night outside. Dark and sleepy time and they sleep and say they will sleep and sleep again, sleep here where it is sometimes warm and sometimes cold, but always safe. Sleep and wait. Sleep and wait. And put on their house another kind of door. A door that opens in and out. A door that swings open whenever you walk up to it. No lock. No key. No slam. And now I'll say goodbye," Dibs added, standing in front of me, looking up earnestly. "Keep remembering," he said. "Will return later!"

"Yes," I replied. "You will come back again later. I'll keep remembering."

Dibs noticed a little animal cut-out in the waste basket. "I want this," he said, picking it up. "May I have it?"

"Yes," I said.

Dibs put it in his pocket. "Say 'Yes, Dibs, you may take it home. If it's what *you*, Dibs, want, then that's all right.' "

"Yes, Dibs, you may take it home," I repeated, after him. "If its what *you* want Dibs then that's all right."

Dibs smiled. He reached out and patted my hand. "That's *good!*" he said. He opened the door, took one step out into the hall, then came back and looked at my wristwatch. He reached over and closed the door with a bang. "No," he said. "It isn't time. It is on the fifteen of four. I wait until the church bells ring!"

"You came earlier today, so you leave earlier," I said.

"You have been here a full hour."

Dibs looked steadily at me for a long minute. "My coming time was sooner, but my going time will be the same," he announced.

"No. The going time is earlier, too, today," I said.

"Oh, no," Dibs said. "I come earlier, but I do not go earlier."

"Yes, you do," I said. "Because today you are going to the doctor's. Remember?"

"Remembering that has nothing to do with it," he said.

"You just don't want to go now," I said. "But. . . ."

"That's right," Dibs interrupted to say. He gave me a long, measured look.

"You're not quite sure about it?" I asked.

Dibs sighed. "I guess I am sure. Okay, I'll go, now. And I just hope that doctor sticks his needle in Dorothy and I hope he hurts her until she screams and screams. And inside me I'll laugh and be glad she feels the hurt. And I'll pretend like it doesn't bother me at all. Goodbye. I'll see you next Thursday."

Dibs walked down the hall and into the reception room where his mother and Dorothy were waiting for him. He ignored his sister, took his mother's hand, left the Center without a word to anyone.

Chapter Ten

WHEN DIBS CAME in the following week he walked back to the playroom with easy, relaxed steps. He paused by the door, turned the little sign on the door. "Do not disturb, please," he said.

He entered the playroom, took off his hat and coat and hung them on the doorknob. He sat down on the ledge of the sandbox and removed his shoes. He put them on the floor beneath his coat. He collected the four guns that had been placed around the room and took them into the puppet theater. He came out, got his hat and coat and took them into the puppet theater. He came out, picked up a toy airplane with a broken propeller. He sat down at the table and very quietly and efficiently repaired the broken propeller.

He got the box of farm animals, sorted through the figures, naming the animals. Then he went to the sandbox, climbed in, examined the little house that was in there.

"You know, I saw a little house just like this in a hardware store on Lexington Avenue," he announced.

"You did?" I said.

"Yes, I did," he replied. "It was exactly like this one. The same size. The same color. Made of metal. Two dollars and ninety-eight cents. That was the price." He turned the house around. "They come all flattened out in a box. Then you put them together. It was exactly like this." He rapped with his fingers on the metal. "It's a thin piece of metal," he said.

He looked at the radiator. "It is warm in here today,"

he said. "I'll turn off the radiator." He leaned over and turned off the radiator.

"There were many toys in the hardware store," he said. "There was a little truck very much like this one." He held one of the little trucks up for me to see. "A dump truck with a little handle that you can crank up so it will dump out the sand."

"A truck like that one?"

Dibs seemed to be stalling for time for some reason or other. But he seemed to be very relaxed. "Quite a lot like this one. But not exactly so. I would say it was almost the same size. And the mechanism was like this one. But it was not painted the same color—and it had a name printed on the side. It was made of heavier metal. They were asking one dollar and seventy-five cents for the one in the store."

He filled the little truck with sand, cranked the handle, elevated the body of the truck, dumped out the sand, cranked it down to a starting position and repeated this activity several times. A mound of sand started to take shape in front of him as he did this. "It will make a hill for me to climb," he said. "I could play the men are going fighting."

He jumped out of the sandbox, hurried across the playroom, picked up the drum. He sat down on the ledge of the sandbox and beat upon the drum with the drumsticks. "Funny, funny drum," he said. "Oh drum, so full of sounds. Slow sounds. Fast sounds. Soft sounds. Beat—beat goes the drum. Fight—fight—fight says the beat—beat goes the drum. Fight—fight—fight says the drum. Come—come—come—come says the drum. Follow me. Follow me. Follow me." He placed the drum carefully on the ledge of the sandbox, climbed back into the sand, began to build a hill in the sand.

"I'm going to start to work, now," he said. "I am going to build a high hill. A high, high hill. And the soldiers all fight to get up to the top of that hill. They so *want* to get up that hill." He quickly built his hill, selected some toy soldiers and placed them in various positions, seemingly climbing up the hill.

"They really do seem to want to get up to the top of that hill, don't they?" I said.

"Oh, yes," Dibs replied. "They really do."

He gathered together all the toy soldiers he could find. He placed them all around the hill he had made. "I'll take more and more soldiers," he said. "I'll let them try to get up that hill—up to the very top of that hill. Because they know what is up there on the very top of that hill if they could only make it to the top. And they do so want to get to the top."

He looked at me. His eyes were shining. "Know what is at the top of that hill?" he asked.

"No. What is?" I asked.

Dibs laughed, knowingly, but kept his own counsel. He inched each soldier up slowly toward the top. But after he had moved all the soldiers a fraction of an inch toward the goal, he sifted more sand on the top of his hill and made it a little higher. He then turned each soldier and slowly, one by one, brought them back down. One by one, he marched them into the little metal house, standing in the sandbox.

"They were not able to get to the top today," he said. "They all go back into their house. They turn and wave. Sadly, they wave. They had wanted to get to the top of that hill. But no one of them could do it today."

"And they felt sad, did they, because they couldn't do what they so wanted to do?" I commented.

"Yes," Dibs sighed. "They wanted to. And they tried. But they couldn't quite do it. But they did find their mountain. And they did climb it. Up. Up. Up. Quite a way! And for a while they *thought* they would get up to the top. And while they *thought* they could, they were happy."

"Just trying to get to the top of the hill made them happy?" I asked.

"Yes," Dibs said. "It's like that with hills. Did you ever climb a hill?"

"Yes. And you, Dibs?" I asked.

"Yes. Once I did. I didn't get to the top of it," he added

wistfully. "But I stood at the bottom of it and looked up. I think every child should have a hill all his own to climb. And I think every child should have one star up in the sky that is all his own. And I think every child should have a tree that belongs to him. That's what I *think* should be," he added, and he looked at me and nodded with emphasis, as he spoke.

"Those things seem important to you, do they?" I asked.

"Yes," he answered. "Very important."

He picked up the metal shovel and quietly and intently dug a deep hole in the sand. Then I noticed that he had selected and set apart one of the toy soldiers. When he had finished digging the hole, he carefully placed that soldier in the bottom of the hole and shoveled sand in on top of it. When the grave was filled in he slapped the top of it with the back of the shovel. "This one just got buried," he announced. "This one did not get a chance to even try to climb that hill. And of course, he did not get to the top. Oh, he wanted to. He wanted to be with the others. He wanted to hope too. He wanted to try. But he didn't get a chance. He got buried."

"So that one got buried," I commented. "He didn't get a chance to climb up the hill. And he didn't get to the top."

"He got buried," Dibs told me, leaning toward me as he spoke. "And not only did he get buried, but I will build another big, high, powerful hill on the top of that grave. He will never, never, never get out of that grave. He will never, never, never have a chance to climb any hill again!" He scooped up the sand with broad sweeps of his hands and built a hill over the grave he had made—over the grave of the buried toy soldier. When the hill was completed, he brushed the sand from his hands, sat there cross-legged, looking at it. "That one was Papa," he said quietly, climbing out of the sandbox.

"It was Papa who got buried under the hill?"

"Yes," Dibs replied. "It was Papa."

The church chimes rang. Dibs counted the chimes as

they struck the hour. "One. Two. Three. Four. Four o'clock," he said. "I have a clock at home and can tell time."

"You have?" I replied. "And you can tell time, too."

"Yes," he said. "There are many different kinds of clocks. Some you wind. Some are electric. Some have alarms. Some play chimes."

"And what kind is yours?" I asked. Dibs seemed to be retreating from the burial of "Papa" by this intellectual discourse. I would go along with him. It would take time for him to work through these feelings about his father. If he seemed to feel that he was getting in over his head, if he seemed to be a little frightened by what he had just played out, and if he sought for himself a retreat into the safety of a discussion about some material things—like clocks—I would not rush him into any probing of his feelings. He had already made some very concise, affective statements in his play.

"Mine is an alarm clock with chimes," he said. "I wind it. I also have a wristwatch. And a clock radio."

He picked up the drum and beat is slowly. "I beat the drum for Papa," he said.

"So those slow drum beats are for Papa?" I commented.

"Yes," said Dibs.

"What does the drum say now?" I asked.

Dibs beat the drum, slowly and deliberately. "Sleep. Sleep. Sleep," he said. "Sleep. Sleep Sleep. Sleep, SLERP SLERPS.LERPS.LERPS.LERPS.LERP!" As he called out each letter, he gradually increased the tempo. He ended with a flourish of beats on the drum.

Dibs sat there, with bent head. The drum was silent. Then he arose and quietly placed the drum in the puppet theater and closed the door. "Put you in here, drum," he said. "Put the drum in here in this closet and shut the door." He walked back to the sandbox and stood there, looking down at the hill-covered grave.

Then he went into the puppet theater and closed the door behind him. There was a small window inside this tricornered theater, which looked out over the parking lot.

From this window, Dibs could see the back of the church.
I could not see Dibs, but I heard him speak plainly.

"There is the back of the church," he said. "The big,
big, church. The church that goes up to the sky. The
church that makes music. The church that chimes—one,
two, three, four, when it is four o'clock. A big church,
with bushes of sticks around it. And where people go."
There was a long interval of silence. Then he continued to
speak. "And sky. So lots of sky away up there. And a
bird. And airplane. And smoke." There was another long
pause. "And Dibs standing by a little window, looking out
at the bigness."

"It looks like a big, big world to you from here," I
commented.

"That's right," he said, softly. "Bigness. Just bigness!"

"Everything seems so very, very big," I said.

Dibs came out of the puppet theater. He sighed. "But
not Dibs," he said. "Dibs isn't church-size."

"Everything is so big, it makes Dibs feel little?" I said.

Dibs climbed back into the sandbox. "In here, I'm
big," he said. "I'll take down the hill. I'll flat it out." He
did. He leveled the mountain. He sifted the sand through
his fingers. "Oh, flattened hill," he said. "Oh, flattened
mountain!"

He looked at me and smiled. "We went to the shoe
repairman's shop after Papa's shoes," he said. "We went
down on Lexington Avenue. We went down Seventy-
second Street. There were buses and taxis and on Third
Avenue, there were tracks overhead. We could have taken
the bus. We could have taken a taxi. We could have
walked. But we didn't. We took our own car."

"You could have gone several different ways, but you
went in your car?"

Dibs leaned closer to me. His eyes were twinkling. "Oh,
don't you forget," he chided gently. "We got *Papa's*
shoes!"

"Oh, yes," I said. "I mustn't forget that you got Papa's
shoes."

"The shoe man fixed them," Dibs said.

"They had been mended?"

"Fixed and mended," Dibs said. "Even repaired!"

"Well, Dibs," I said. "It is time to go now."

"It is time to go," Dibs agreed. He stood up. "Time to go five minutes ago?"

Dibs was so right. I had not wanted to interrupt his account of the trip after "Papa's" shoes by announcing the time. "Yes, you are right," I said. "It is five minutes past the time."

Dibs got his hat and coat out of the puppet theater. "This is a funny closet," he said, when he came out, putting on his hat and coat. "A funny closet with a hole in the door and a window in it." He crossed the room and picked up his shoes. "These are new shoes," he said. He sat down and put them on without assistance. Before he put his shoes on, he stuck both feet out toward me. "See?" he said. "New socks, too. No holes. Mother was so embarrassed at the doctor's." He laughed. He tied his shoelaces neatly and tightly. He stood up. As he went out the door he stopped, turned the little sign. "They can disturb," he said. "We are gone."

Chapter Eleven

WHEN DIBS RETURNED the following Thursday, he entered the playroom briskly. He took off his hat and coat and flung them on a chair. "Miss A's office is number twelve," he announced. "And this room is seventeen. And this chair has a number on the back of it. Number thirteen. See it?" He quickly turned the chair, tapped the number with his finger.

"That's right," I commented. At times, he seemed a stickler for precise detail.

He walked over to the cupboard and selected the box containing the little buildings of a toy village. He sat down on the floor and sorted through the miniature houses, stores, factories, churches, and other buildings. There were tiny trees to place throughout the constructed villages. Dibs was completely absorbed with this material. "This is a toy village," he said. "Let's see what we have here. Churches. Houses. Trees. I will build a village with these," he commented. "Here are two churches. I will start with the churches. I will make this taller church the center of my little village. And I'll put this little church over here. Then I'll select my houses and line them up in neat rows of streets. This is to be a small town, so there can be more space around the houses. And small towns and little villages always have churches. See the steeple on the church? This will be a whole world of houses."

He lay down on the floor, with his cheek pressed against the linoleum. He moved a few of the buildings. "I created this little town," he said. "I have made here a little world of houses. I have planted the trees around it. I have imagined the sky and the rain and the gentle winds. I have dreamed up the seasons. And now I'll call forth the spring. The trees are growing into leaves. It is nice and beautiful and comfortable in this quiet little town. There are people walking down the street. The trees grow silently along the way. The trees are different. The trees have different kinds of bark on their trunks."

He rolled over and looked at me. "Ask me if I have any more houses," he said.

"Do you have any more houses?" I asked.

"I have used up all the houses," said Dibs. "There are none left." He placed more of the trees around his village.

"This tree has green edges," he said. "It stands here, pointing up, up, up to the sky. It whispers secrets as the winds pass by. Tell me where you have been? Tell me what you have seen? For I have roots that tie me to the earth and I must stand forever here. And the wind whispers back 'I never stay. I blow away. Away today. Away, Away. Away,' I say. Away. And the tree cries out 'I want to go with you. I don't want to stand here, alone and sad. I want to go with you. You seem so glad.' Oh, well. . . ."

Dibs got up and walked over to the table. He picked up a puzzle that had been left there. He sat down on the floor at my feet and quickly put the pieces together. "It is Tom Tom The Piper's Son," he said. "We have a song at school about it. I will sing it to you." Dibs sang the song, words and melody correctly done. "The end," he announced, when he had finished.

"You learned that at school, did you?" I asked.

"Yes," he replied. "Miss Jane is my teacher. Miss Jane is a grown-up woman. Miss A is a grown-up woman. There are grown-ups and grown-ups."

"Grown-ups seem to differ from one another, do they?" I asked.

"Indeed, they do!" Dibs said, emphatically.

"Do you know any other grown-ups?" I asked.

"Of course, I do," said Dibs. "There is Hedda. And some others at the school. And there is Jake, our gardener. And there is Millie who does our laundry. And Jake trimmed one of the big trees in our yard at home. It was the tree outside my window and it grew close enough for me to reach out my window and touch it. But Papa wanted it trimmed. He said it rubbed against the house. And I watched Jake climb up the tree, sawing off bran-ches of the tree. I opened my window and I told him that tree was my friend and that branch I needed and I told him I didn't want it cut off. And Jake didn't cut it off. And then Papa went out and said he wanted it *off* because it was too close to the house and it spoiled the shape of the tree. Jake said I liked that branch, because it was so close I could reach out my window and touch it. Then Papa said he wanted it cut off, anyway. Papa said he didn't want me hanging out the window. He said he didn't know I had been doing that and he said he would put a safety screen of heavy metal on the window so I couldn't fall out. Then he told Jake to cut off the branch and be quick about it. And Jake said he could cut a little off, so it wouldn't rub the house because Jake said I *liked* that branch. And Papa said I had plenty of other things to play with. He made Jake saw it off, so far away from the window I couldn't ever reach it. But Jake saved me the tip end of the branch that I used to touch. Jake told me I could keep that part of the tree *inside* my room—that not every tree had a chance to have its favorite branch live in a house. He told me it was an old, old elm tree. He said it was probably two hundred years old and in all that time probably no one had ever loved it as much as I did. So I kept the tip-end branch. I still have it."

"When did this happen?" I asked.

"A year ago," Dibs said, "But Jake couldn't help it. He had to cut off that branch. Then they put the safety screen on the window. They had a man come out and do it. He put one on my window and one on Dorothy's window."

"Did anyone know Jake gave you that tip-end branch?" I asked.

"I don't know. I never told anyone. I just kept it. I've

still got it. I won't let anyone touch it. I'd kick and bite anybody who tried."

"That branch meant a lot to you, didn't it?"

"Oh, yes," Dibs answered.

"Did you spend very much time with Jake?" I asked.

"Yes. Every time I could go out in the yard I'd stay with Jake. He talked to me. I would listen to everything he said. He told me all kinds of stories. He told me about St. Francis of Assisi. He lived a long time ago and he loved birds and trees and the wind and the rain, too. He said they were friends. And they are, too. Nicer than people," Dibs added, with emphasis.

He walked around the playroom restlessly. "I watch the tree," he said. "Still, I watch the tree. In the spring the leaves come out, and open up, and grow green because the rain has brought them green life again. And they open up because of their gladness in it being spring again. And all summer they give friendly, cool shade. Then, in winter, the leaves blow away. Jake says in the fall the wind comes after them and takes them away on trips around the world. He told me a story once about the last leaf that was left on that tree. He said the little leaf was sad because it thought it had been forgotten and it would never be free to go anyplace. But the wind came back after that one lonely little leaf and blew it on one of the most wonderful trips anyone had ever had. He said the little leaf was blown all around the world and had seen all the wonderful things there are in the world. And when it had gone all around the world, it came back to our yard, Jake said, because it missed me. And Jake found it back under our tree one winter day. It was all tired and thin and worn from its long trip. But Jake said it had wanted to come back to me because it hadn't met anybody else in all the world it liked as much as it liked me. So Jake gave it to me." Dibs took another restless turn around the room. He pause in front of me. "I keep that leaf," he said. "It is very tired and very old. But I keep that leaf. I mounted it and framed it. And I imagine some of the things it must have seen, flying all around the world with the wind. And I read in my books about the countries it saw."

He walked over to the doll house. "I'll lock it up," he said. "I'll lock the door and I'll close all the windows."

"Why, Dibs?" I asked. "Why do *you* want to lock the door and close the windows?"

"I don't know," Dibs muttered.

He walked back to me. "My shoe," he said, with a trace of the old whimper of helplessness in his voice. "Tie my shoelace for me, Miss A."

"All right, Dibs. I'll tie it for you." I did. He picked up the nursing bottle and sucked on it. He sighed.

"Are you feeling sort of sad?" I asked.

He nodded his head. "Sad," he said.

"Does Jake still do your gardening?"

"No. Not any more," Dibs said. "Papa said he was too old and it isn't good for him to work like that since his heart attack. But he still comes around once in a while. We visit, out in the yard. He always tells me a story. But he hasn't been around for a long time. I miss him."

"Yes, I'm sure you do, Dibs," I said. "Jake must be a very nice person."

"Oh, he is," Dibs said. "I like him very, very much. I guess, maybe, he is a friend?" he asked wistfully.

"I'd guess he is a friend, Dibs," I answered. "A very, very good friend."

Dibs walked over to the window and looked out for a long time in silence. "Jake went to church every Sunday," he said, pointing out toward the church. "He told me he did."

"Did you ever go to church, Dibs?" I asked.

"Oh, no," Dibs said, quickly. "Papa and Mother are not church-believing people. Therefore, neither Dorothy nor I are church-believers."

"I see," I commented.

"But Jake is. And Grandmother," Dibs said.

Again there was silence.

"Ten more minutes?" Dibs asked.

"No," I said.

"Nine more minutes?" he asked.

"No," I said.

"Eight more?" Dibs asked.

"Yes. Eight more minutes."

"Then, I'll play with the doll family and the house the rest of the time," Dibs answered. He picked up a package of writing paper. "I'll put this in my house," he said. He placed it in one of the rooms of the doll house. "Someone fixed on the door again," he said.

"Yes."

He pointed to the attic of the house. "That's the attic room," he said.

"Yes. It could be," I commented.

"Get the grown-ups all ready for bed," he said, selecting the dolls and placing them in the bedrooms. "And now the children. That's the baby. And the cook, here. And the laundress. The laundress says she is tired. She wants to rest. Here are the beds. This is the father's room. You must not go in there. You must not bother him. He is busy. And this is the man's bed. This is the mother's room. This is her bed. And each child has a bed of his own. And each has a room of his own. The cook has her room and her bed. She says she gets tired, too. And the laundress doesn't have a bed. She has to stand up and watch the machines and this child sometimes goes down to the laundry and he asks her why she doesn't go to bed and rest if she is tired and she says they pay her to work not to rest. But Mother says she can have a rocking chair down there. No reason why she couldn't rock if she wants to. She has been washing for this family forty years. She can rock once in a while, for heaven's sake, can't she? the cook says. But she says not if the rocker squeaks, she can't, because it would bother the man and God help us if we bother the man, she says. But the cook says let him go soak his old head in the soapsuds. Then she sends the boy upstairs and says there aren't enough fancy things in the laundry for him. So he goes back upstairs."

At this moment, I accidentally kicked the puzzle Dibs

had put together on the floor at my feet. I bent down and straightened it. Dibs glanced at me quickly.

"What are you doing?" he asked.

"I kicked your puzzle and Tom Tom the Piper's Son came apart," I said.

Dibs looked at me curiously. "What did you say?" he asked. "I didn't understand what you said then."

"I said I accidentally kicked your puzzle and Tom Tom the Piper's Son came apart," I told him.

"Oh," said Dibs. He was certainly well aware of every movement that took place in this room, no matter how engrossed he seemed to be in his own activity. He dropped down on his knees and looked to see if I had fixed it correctly. It passed inspection. He stood up and played with the lock on the playroom door. "Lock it?" he asked.

"Do you want the door locked?" I asked.

"That's right," Dibs said. He locked the door. "It is locked," he said.

After a moment had passed, I added, "Yes. Now it is locked. Now, let me see you unlock it; because now it is time to go home."

"That's right," Dibs said. "Even if *you* know I don't want to go home."

"Yes. Even if I know you don't *feel* like going home, there are times, Dibs, when you have to. And this is one of those times."

He stood in front of me, looking steadily into my eyes. He sighed. "Yes," he said. "I know. So much I can do here, but then, always, I finally must go." He started out the door.

"You hat and coat," I said.

"Yes. Your hat and coat," he said. He went back, picked up his coat and put it on. He crammed his hat down on his head. "*My* hat and coat," he said. He looked at me. "Goodbye, Miss A. Thursday will come again. Every week has a Thursday. Goodbye." He walked down the hall to the reception room. I watched him go. He turned back, waved his hand, "Goodbye," he said again.

So young. So small. And yet so full of strength. Then I thought of Jake and wondered if he knew how much his understanding and gentle kindness had become such an important part of the development of this young child. I thought of that symbolic tip-end branch and the thin, tired, worn little leaf. I thought of Dibs' wistful question:

"I guess, maybe, he is a friend?"

Chapter Twelve

EVERY WEEK HAS A THURSDAY and the week that followed was no exception. However, Dibs was not able to come to the playroom. He had the measles. His mother telephoned and cancelled the appointment. By the following Thursday he had recovered sufficiently and appeared promptly for his play therapy session. His face was still blotched and pale but as he came into the reception room, he announced, "The measles are all gone. I am better now."

"You're all over the measles, now, are you?" I commented, seeing, but not believing this time.

"Yes," Dibs said. "Over and done with them. Let's go back to the playroom."

As we walked past my office, Dibs looked in. Two men were repairing recording machines in my office. "There are two men in our office," he said. "I mean there are two men in your office."

"Yes. They will be working in there while we are in the playroom," I told him.

"You let other people in your office?" he asked.

"Yes. Sometimes I do."

"What are they doing in there?" he asked.

"They are repairing some of the recording machines."

As we entered the playroom, Dibs took off his hat and coat and threw them down on a chair. "I missed last Thursday," he said.

"Yes, I know. I'm sorry you had the measles and couldn't come," I said.

"I got the card you sent me," he said. "It made me happy. I liked getting the card."

"I'm glad you did," I replied.

"It said to hurry and get well. It said you missed me."

"Yes, it did."

"I liked the pussywillows you sent me. They were like the spring. Nice pussywillows. With big pussykittens on each branch. I liked them. Papa said they would get roots after a long time in water and I could plant them in the yard. He said they *might* grow into bushes. Could that happen?" Dibs asked.

"You said your papa told you that. So what do you think?" I asked.

"I expect he is correct," Dibs said. "But I'll watch for myself and try it and see."

"That is a way of finding out things," I said.

I was interested in Dibs' reference to his father's remark. It was difficult to know whether this conversation was a new approach to Dibs by his father—or whether his father had many times attempted to explain things to Dibs even though he had received no consistent response from Dibs. As Miss Jane had done at the school. As Jake may have done so many times when Dibs "just listened." Now, however, Dibs was reporting it to me in a very matter-of-fact way.

"What did you say when your papa told you about the pussywillows?" I asked, hoping to pick up another fragment of understanding.

"I didn't say anything," Dibs replied. "I just listened."

He walked around the playroom, looking at the paint jars, at the materials on the table. Then he went to the sandbox and jumped into the sand with a free, spontaneous movement. He lay down full length. "Want to take your shoes off, Dibs?" he asked himself. "No," he answered. "Well, what *do* you want to do, Dibs?" he asked. "Make up your mind!" He rolled over and stuck his face down against the sand. "I'm in no hurry," he said. "For now, I'll just be!" He pushed his hands down through the sand and pulled out some of the little buildings that had been buried in the sand by some other child. "Oh, I am finding things in the sand. Little buildings. Little odds and ends. Things." Then, suddenly, he went down to the other end of the sandbox and began to dig in the sand. Finally, his shovel scraped the metal bottom of the box. Dibs reached down in the sand and pulled out a toy soldier. He held it aloft.

"Oh, la, la! This man!" he exclaimed. "See here? See this fighting man? This was the man I buried beneath my mountain. I am happy to find he is still buried all these weeks. Now back you go, sir! Back you go! Back into your grave again!" He reburied the little toy soldier. As he did, he began to sing:

Oh, do you know the muffin man,
The muffin man, the muffin man,
Oh, do you know the muffin man
That lies in Dreary Lane.

He looked at me. He grinned. "I learned that song at school," he said. "Now, I'll sing it for the buried man":

Oh, did you know the nothing man,
The nothing man, the nothing man,
Oh, did you know the nothing man?
He lives in a dreary grave.

Dibs laughed. He smacked the top of the grave with the shovel for emphasis.

"No," he said to me, very casually, as though there had been no time lag between my question and this answer. "I don't talk much to Papa."

"You don't?"

"No."

"Why don't you?" I asked.

"I don't know," Dibs replied, "I guess it's because I just don't."

He hummed another melody, "I learned that one at school, too," he said.

"Do you sing that at school, too?" I asked.

"I learned it at school," Dibs said, "I sing it here, to you."

"Oh," I replied.

Asking questions in therapy would be so helpful if anyone ever answered them accurately. But no one ever does. I often wondered if there had been any changes in Dibs' behavior at school. Apparently, there had not been any very noticeable changes, because the teachers had not reported any. That had been our agreement. But Dibs was learning many things in school, at home, everywhere he went, even though he might not behave in such a way that his learning could be evaluated or tested.

"Take off your shoes, Dibs," he told himself. He removed his shoes. He filled them with sand, shoveling the sand with elaborate motions. Then he took off one sock and filled it with sand. He pulled the side of his other sock out from his leg and shoveled the sand in, between sock and leg. Then he took the sock off and stuck his feet down under the sand. He shoveled the sand on top of his feet until a mound of sand buried his feet and the lower part of his legs.

Suddenly, he pulled his feet out of the sand, stood up, jumped out of the sandbox, and opened the playroom door. He reached up, took the card out of the holder, came back into the room, closed the door, thrust the card at me.

"What is therapy?" he asked me.

I was astonished. "Therapy?" I said. "Well, let me think for a minute." Why had he asked this question, I wondered. What explanation would make a sensible reply?

"I would say that it means a chance to come here and play and talk just about any way you want to," I said. "It's a time when you can be the way you want to be. A time when you can use it. A time when you can use anyway you want to use it. A time when you can be you." That was the best explanation I could come up with then. He took the card out of my hand. He turned it to the other side.

"I know what this means," he said. "Do not disturb."

means everybody please let them alone. Don't bother them. Don't knock on the door, either. Just let them both be. This side means *they are being*. And this side says *you let them both be!* Like that?"

"Yes. Like that."

Someone walked down the hall. Dibs heard their footsteps. "Someone is walking down the hall," he said. "But this is our room. They won't come in here, will they?"

"I don't think they will," I said.

"This is just for me, isn't it?" Dibs asked. "Just for me. Not for anyone else."

"It's just for you at this time every week if you want it that way," I said.

"For Dibs and Miss A," said Dibs. "Not just for me. For you, too."

"For both of us, then," I said.

Dibs opened the door. "I'll put the sign up again," he said. "They shall not disturb." He replaced the card, patted the door, came back in, and closed the door. There was a happy smile on his face. He walked over to the easel.

"Dibs, now that you are out of the sandbox, don't you think you should put your shoes and socks on?" I asked.

"That's right," Dibs said. "What with my measles and all. But *first* my socks and then my shoes."

"Oh, yes. Of course. I said your shoes and socks, didn't I?" I replied.

"That's right," Dibs said. He smiled. Then, after his socks and shoes were on again, and the shoelaces securely tied he got back into the sand. "When I had measles on me I had to stay in bed," he said. "And they kept the window shades down and the room was as dark as they could make it. And I couldn't read, or draw, or write."

"Then what did you do?" I asked.

"They played records for me. And mother told me some stories. I have lots of stories on records and I listened to them all over again. But I like my music records best."

"The stories and the music must have helped pass the time, didn't they?" I commented.

"But I missed my books," Dibs said.

"You like to read, don't you?" I said.

"Oh, yes. Very, very much. And I like to write stories about what I see and what I think. I like to draw pictures, too. But I like to read best of all."

"What do you like to read?" I asked. "What kind of books do you have?"

"Oh, I have all kinds of books. I have books about birds and animals and trees and plants and rocks and fish and people and stars and the weather and countries and two sets of encyclopedias and a dictionary—my picture dictionary that I've had for a long, long time. And the giant, full-sized dictionary that used to be Papa's. I have several long shelves of books. And books of poems. And some old story books. But I like the science books best. But better than any of them, I liked the card you sent me. They did let me have that in bed with me. They let me open it. Mother let me read it first. And let me keep it and read it again and again."

"I suppose you have spent a lot of your time reading, haven't you?" I said.

"Oh yes. Lots of times that's all I ever did," Dibs said. "But I like it. I like to read about the things I see. Then I like to see the things I read about. I have all kinds of rocks and leaves and mounted insects and butterflies. And batteries and cameras. I sometimes take pictures of things in the yard. And in the tree outside my window. Only my pictures aren't very good. I draw better ones. But I like your playroom better," he added, nodding his head for emphasis.

"You like this one better? They are quite different, aren't they?" I said.

"Oh yes," Dibs said. "So very different."

"In what ways are they different?" I asked. I couldn't resist pursuing this topic.

"Just like you said," Dibs said quite seriously. "They are quite different that way."

I let it drop. All this additional detail was interesting, but it did not explain in what manner Dibs had learned to read and write and spell and draw. According to all the existing learning theories, he should not have been able to have achieved any of these skills without having first mastered verbal language and without having had appropriate background experiences. Nevertheless, Dibs did possess these skills to an advanced degree.

The weekly truck drove up and stopped outside the playroom window. "Look out the window," Dibs said. He did. He watched while the men unloaded the truck. He watched the men get into the truck and drive away. He opened the window and leaned out, watching the truck until it disappeared. Then he closed the window.

The church chimes began to play. Dibs turned and looked at me. "Oh, listen," he said. "It's going to be four o'clock. Right now!" He counted the chimes. "One. Two. Three. Four. How much longer?" he asked.

"Fifteen more minutes," I said.

"Oh?" Dibs said. He counted his fingers like a miser, up to fifteen, slowly, laboriously. "Fifteen?" he asked. "Five minutes and ten minutes? Ten minutes and five minutes?"

"Yes," I said.

"Sometimes minutes are happy," he said. "And sometimes they are sad. There are sad times and happy times."

"Yes. Some times are sad and some happy," I replied.

"I'm happy now," Dibs said.

"You are?"

"Yes. Happy."

He opened the window and leaned out. "Oh, beautiful day!" he said. "Oh, happy day. With sky so blue. And birds flying. Oh, hear that airplane? Oh, happy sky. Oh, happy, west-flying airplane. Oh, happy bird. Oh, happy Dibs. Oh, Dibs, with the pussywillow branches to plant and to watch grow! Oh, tell me Dibs, how happy are you?" He turned and looked at me. Then he turned back to the open window. "So happy I'll even spit out the window before I close it again!" he exclaimed. And he did.

"When the bells ring again, it will be time to go," I said.

"Oh," said Dibs. He came over to me and quickly, silently touched my hand. Then he walked over to the easel. He quickly re-arranged the order of the paints. He got the box of farm animals. He took out the pieces for the fence and examined them. "I'll make a nice farm," he announced. He began to sing:

Oh, I'll make a farm!
A happy farm!
A farm for you and me!

He looked at me. "How many more minutes left?" he asked. I wrote the number five on a piece of paper and held it out for him to see. He looked at it, and laughed. He took my pencil, waited a few seconds, wrote a four, waited a second, then wrote a three, waited another second, wrote a two, waited a second, wrote a one, "Time to go home," he shouted. "Only the church bells haven't rung yet."

"You got there ahead of the bells," I commented.

"Yes, I did," he said. He looked down at the fence he had erected across the floor. "See?" he said, pointing to the fence.

"It's a long fence," I said.

"Oh, say! Isn't it long!" he said. He began to sing again:

I built a fence,
A fence so long
It's end I couldn't see.
Why is a fence?
Where is a fence?
I don't want one for me!

He laughed. "I'll put the farm animals inside the fence," he announced. He placed a horse and a cow behind the fence. "Now this cow," he said, holding it up for me to see. "This cow gives milk. It is a friendly cow. All the cows stand in a row, ready to give milk." Then he spoke in a sharp voice. "Get in line, cow. Straighten up. You heard me speak to you. Don't act like such a stupid idiot!"

He held up the rooster. "This is the rooster," he said. The chimes began to play.

"Listen, Dibs," I said.

"Yes," said Dibs. "One o'clock. Three more hours until four."

"Oh, come now, Dibs," I said. "Are you trying to fool me? Isn't it time to go home?"

"Yes, it is," Dibs said. "But let's pretend."

"Pretend?"

"Yes. Let's pretend it's one o'clock," he said.

"Would pretending really change this time?" I asked him.

"Well, no," Dibs said. "There are two kinds of pretending."

"And what are they?" I asked.

"The pretending that is all right to pretend," he said. "And the pretending that is just plain foolish." He stood up and walked over to me. "And sometimes they get so mixed up you can't tell which is which," he added. "I'm going to stop by the doctor's now. In fact, we were on our way to the doctor's when we came here today. We came here first, though, because I wanted to come so much and mother was sure it was all right because she said she had asked you and you said you had had the measles. But maybe the doctor would have said no." He put on his hat and coat. "But I am all right," he assured me. "I can't give anybody measles, now." He grinned happily. "Good-bye," he said. "I expect I'll see you next Thursday." He left.

And I was left with my speculations and the inferences I might draw from some of this conversation with Dibs.

He seemed to be more at ease in his relationship with his mother. There were indications that Dibs was being treated with more consideration, understanding, and respect at home. Even "Papa" seemed to be emerging as more of a person. But were they changing in their behavior towards Dibs? Or had Dibs changed in his capacity to relate to his mother and father so that he could receive their advances toward him more naturally?

Certainly they had provided ample material things to feed his keen intellectual capacities. Certainly, they had attempted to communicate with him and to teach him many things. It was exceedingly difficult to understand how they could have felt this child was mentally defective when they had been providing materials far beyond the capacities of an average child of Dibs' age. Certainly they must have known that Dibs' problem was not due to any lack of intellectual ability. But why did he still maintain these two completely different types of behavior—one so gifted and superior, the other so woefully deficient?

Chapter Thirteen

DIBS SEEMED QUITE HAPPY when he returned to the playroom the following week. "Mother might be late getting back today," he said.

"Yes, I know. She told me that she might," I replied.

"She has gone on an errand," Dibs said. "She said I could wait here for her until she got back. She said she had arranged it with you."

"That's right," I said.

He walked around the playroom with a smile on his face. "I think I will sing," he announced.

"If you want to sing, you sing," I replied. He laughed.

"And if I want to be quiet, I be quiet!" he exclaimed. "And if I want to think, I just think. And if I want to play, I play. Like that, h'mm?"

"Yes. Like that," I said.

He walked over to the easel and looked at the paints. He picked up the jar of blue paint. He started to sing, and as he sang, he held up the jar of paint and moved it rhythmically, from side to side.

> Oh, paint! Oh, paint so blue!
> What, oh what, is it you can do?
> You can paint a sky.
> You can paint a river.
> You can paint a flower.
> You can paint a bird.
> All things are blue
> If you make them blue.
> Oh, blue paint, oh, paint, so blue!

He walked up to me with the jar of paint.

It'll spill. It'll slop.
It'll drop. It'll run.
My lovely, blue paint, it will.

He continued singing the words he made up as he went along.

It's a *moving color*.
It moves and moves.
Oh blue! Oh blue! Oh blue!

He swayed the jar of paint back and forth as he sang.
He set it back on the easel and picked up the jar of green paint.

Oh green paint so green.
You are quiet and nice.
Around me in spring.
Around me in summer.
In leaves, in grass, in hedges, too.
Oh, green! Oh, green! Oh, green!

He replaced the green paint and picked up the jar of black paint.

Oh, black! Oh, night!
Oh, sable dark.
Come at me from all around.
Oh shadows and dreams
And storms and night!
Oh, black! Oh, black! Oh, black!

He replaced this jar and picked up the red paint. He brought this over to me, held it up, cupped between his hands. This time he spoke the words emphatically.

Oh red, angry paint.
Oh paint that scowls.
Oh blood so red.
Oh hate. Oh mad. Oh fear.
Oh noisy fights and smeary red.
Oh hate. Oh blood. Oh tears.

He lowered the jar of red paint in his hands. He stood there silently, looking at it. Then he sighed deeply, re-placed it on the easel. He picked up the yellow paint. "Oh mean colored yellow," he said. "Oh angry, mean color. Oh, bars on windows to keep out the tree. Oh door with the lock and the turned key. I hate you, yellow. Mean old color. Color of prisons. Color of being lonely and afraid. Oh mean-colored yellow." He put it back on the easel.

He walked over to the window and looked out. "It's a beautiful day, today," he commented.

"Yes, it is," I replied.

He stood there, looking out the window for a long time. I sat there, wondering why he had projected these associa-tions to the colors of the paint. Why had he shown so much negative association with the yellow paint?

He went back to the easel. "This turquoise paint is new," he said.

"Yes, it is."

He put two large pieces of paper on the easel. He carefully stirred the turquoise paint with a brush. He took the brush to the sink, turned the water on and let it run on the brush. "Oh look!" he said. "It turns the water blue." He placed his fingers over the opening and a fountain of water sprayed out into the room. He shouted with laugh-ter. "The water came out, came out," he cried. "And I, Dibs himself, can make of the water a fountain and can turn the color of the water to blue."

"I see you can," I said.

He dropped the brush and it slipped down the drain. He reached for it quickly, but he could not get it. It was down in the pipe. "Well," he exclaimed. "This is a fine kettle of fish! I can't get it out. Down and out of sight it went. But it is in the pipe. It is in the lower drain." He opened the cupboard doors beneath the sink and examined the pipe. "Too bad!" he said. He laughed heartily.

"Yes. The paintbrush is in the pipe," I said.

He played with the water, turning it on with such force that it splashed out into the room. He got the nursing bottle, filled it. He took the nipple, tried to put it on the bottle, but the wetness made it a slippery impossibility. He chewed the nipple. He set the bottle in the sink and let the water splash down on it. Then he placed the bottle in the drain and the sink began to fill with water. He turned on the drinking fountain that was in the sink, chewed on the nipple, put his face down close to the fountain to wet his face.

"The water is coming up," he announced. "Wash. Wash." He got two empty, dirty paint jars and put them in the sink. Then he noticed the set of plastic dishes on a shelf, removed the paint jars, dumped the plastic dishes into the ink. He jumped up and down and shouted with laughter. "I'll wash the dishes," he cried out. "They are swimming and they get wet. Everything gets wet. It splashes. Where's dish cloth? Where's mat? Where's soap? Splash. Splash. Splash. Oh boy! What fun!"

"You're having lots of fun, aren't you?" I said.

"Yes. It's filling up. It's wet. Some of them are upside down. Get me soap."

I got him some soap and a dish cloth and a towel. He washed the dishes carefully, rinsed them, dried them. "Did you ever see such beautiful dishes?" he asked. "The dishes are like what Grandma sent because Dibs left his toy farm animals with Grandma and she sent them to Dibs by mail."

"Oh?" I said. "Grandma sent you some dishes like these by mail?"

"Yes. I had gone to visit her. I came back home. Grandma forgot to pack my farm animals. So, she mailed them to me. And she put in a surprise. Dishes just like these. Very beautiful dishes exactly like these."

"You liked Grandma sending you the surprise, didn't you?" I commented.

"Yes. Oh, yes! And on May twelfth *Grandma comes home!*" Dibs announced. He looked at me, eyes shining, a big smile on his face. "*Grandma comes home,*" he repeated. "Be glad!" he exclaimed. "May twelfth and grandma comes home."

"I think that makes you feel very, very happy," I said. "You'll be glad to see Grandma, won't you?"

"That's right!" Dibs said. "So glad I could burst." He started to sing again.

To Dibs, with love from Grandma
To Dibs with love, with love.
Grandma comes! Grandma comes!
Grandma comes marching home
With love!

He clapped his hands enthusiastically. "I'm going to have a party," he announced. "Right now. I'm going to have a party." He placed all the little cups in a row. He filled each cup with water. "For all the children," he announced. "For all the children. "For every child, a party. For all the children, a drink. I am having a party. There will be children at my party."

"You are going to have a party for children now?" I said.

"Oh yes. Children. Lots of children. Lots of friendly children."

He counted the cups. "Seven cups," he said. "There will be seven children at my party."

"You are going to have seven children at your party, are you?"

"Six and Dibs," he replied.

"Oh. Six other children and you with them," I said.

"That's right," Dibs said. "Six other children and Dibs makes seven children."

"That's right," I said.

In this play, Dibs was expressing a desire to be one with other children.

The bottle he had used to block the drain slipped and the water gurgled out of the sink. Dibs laughed. "Oh, what a funny noise," he said. "It's four o'clock. It's getting darkish. It's getting late. I'll throw out this water in the cups and refill them for the party drinks. It is time to fill the cups." He filled the plastic pitcher with water and poured water into each cup, singing as he did so. "Oh, cup number one, here's water for you. And cup number two and cup number three. Be careful it spills not, but splash it you can. Cup number four and five and six. Then seven with a splash. Splash. Splash. Splash. Slop. Slop. Slop. Water all over the drainboard. Water all over the floor. Water all over every place. Just one big sloppy splash of water all over every place." He refilled the pitcher and poured the water on the drainboard, on the floor, on the table. As he said, one great big sloppy splash of water all over the place. But he enjoyed every drop of it and every minute of it.

He found two more plastic cups. "Oh, two more cups," he yelled. "There will be nine children at my party. I will have a tea party. I'll have them all for tea. I'll empty the cups and prepare for the tea party." He splashed more water. "Now I'll have my tea party," he said. "How many more minutes?"

"Eight more minutes."

"It'll be an eight-minute tea party," he announced. "We will use our good tea set, today." His tone of voice changed. It became restrained, a little on edge. He imitated perfectly the precise inflection and expression of his mother's voice. "If there is to be a tea party we will do it properly," he said. "Yes. There will be tea. A little tea in each cup, then fill it up with milk. That is too much tea. I said a *little* tea in each cup, then fill it up with milk. If you want more water, that will be all right. But no more tea. And no arguments." He spooned water into each cup. "Cup six has too much tea," he said, with a note of severity in his voice. "Please remove some of the tea from cup six and follow my instructions more accurately. And that is enough sugar for children. *Enough sugar.* It should not be necessary to repeat everything I say. If you want to have a tea party you will sit down quietly at this table and you will wait until everyone is served. You may have a piece of cinnamon toast with your tea. You do not speak with food in your mouth."

Dibs set the table. He drew a chair up to the table. His manner became meek, subdued, quiet as he drank his tea in the little cup.

He picked up the pitcher of water and slowly moved around the table, neatly pouring a little water in each cup. "There will be a little tea in each cup," he said in a tight, precise voice. "That is too much tea in cup three. I'll pour some of it out." Dibs poured out some of the water. "You may have a little sugar in each cup." He busied himself about the table. A second pitcher was designated as the milk. A tiny spoonful of sand was added carefully for the sugar. "Handle the spoonful of sugar with care," Dibs' imitating voice continued. "Cup six has too much tea. That must be corrected. Be careful of the sugar. Children should not have too much sugar. Take your elbows off the table. If there is any more fussing, you will go to your room. I will—lock you—in your room."

Dibs sat down at the table before one of the cups. He folded his hands carefully on the edge of the table. "You must eat the toast carefully," Dibs' voice went on. He reached across for the toast and upset one of the cups. He sprang up from the table, a frightened expression on his face.

"No more party," he cried. "The party is over. I spilled the tea!" Quickly he emptied the cups and returned them to the shelf.

"The party ended because you spilled the tea?" I asked.

"Stupid! Stupid! Stupid!" he cried.

"It was an accident," I said.

"Stupid people make accidents!" he shouted. There

were tears in his eyes. "The party is over. The children are all gone! There is no more party." His voice choked on the tears. This had been a very real experience to him. "It *was* an accident," he told me. "But the party is over."

"It frightened you and made you unhappy," I said. "The accident of spilling the tea ended the party. Did the boy who upset the tea get sent to his room?"

Dibs paced around the playroom, wringing his hands. "He did. Yes. Yes. He should have been careful. It was very stupid of him to be so clumsy." He kicked over a chair. He swept the cups from the shelf. "I didn't want a party," he shouted. "I didn't want any other children around!"

"It makes you angry and unhappy when something like that happens," I said.

Dibs came over to me. "Let's go down to your office," he said. "Let's get out of here. I am not *stupid!*"

"No. You are not stupid," I said. "And it upsets you when something like this happens."

We went down the hall to my office. Dibs sat in the office chair for a long time in silence. Then he looked at me with a little smile on his face. "I'm sorry," he said.

"Sorry? Why are you sorry?" I asked.

"Because I spilled the tea," he said. "I was careless. I shouldn't have been."

"You think you should have been more careful?" I asked.

"Yes," Dibs said. "I should have been more careful, but I am not stupid."

"You were careless, perhaps, but not stupid?"

"That's right," said Dibs. There was a smile on his face.

Dibs had successfully weathered this storm. He had discovered a strength within himself to cope with his hurt feelings.

"I'm going to write a letter," he said. He picked up a pencil and paper and began to print the letter, spelling the words aloud as he wrote.

Dear Dibs:
I washed the tea set and I closed the drain. I had a party. Children were there.
With love.
Me.

He looked at my desk calendar, drew it toward him. He leafed through it until he came to April eighth. He drew a circle around the eighth and wrote his name on that page of the calendar.

"April eighth is my birthday," he said. He leafed through the calendar, singled out another date and wrote "Mother." Then on another dated sheet, he wrote "Papa." Then on another he wrote "Dorothy." "These are the birthdays of Mother, Papa, and Dorothy," he told me. He turned back to the page that had Papa's name printed on it. He wrote "Grandma" on it.

"Papa's birthday and Grandma's birthday are on the same day," he said.

"They are?" I said.

"Yes," Dibs replied, "Only one is older than the other."

"Which one is?" I asked.

"Grandma!" he answered, a note of surprise in his voice. "February twenty-eighth. This is it. Washington's Birthday, too."

"On the twenty-eighth?" I asked.

"No. Washington was born on the twenty-second. Same month, though." He looked down at the page of the calendar. "I'm going to erase this off," he said, pointing to "Papa."

"You are?"

"No," he said, with a sigh, "No. That will have to stay on, because it is his birthday."

"Whether you want it there or not, it is his birthday, h'mm?"

"That's right," Dibs said, "And he needs it."

"What do you mean?" I asked.

"He needs it. I need it," Dibs said.

"Oh," I commented.

"He discovered a blank page in the back of the calendar. "Take this off?" he said.

"If you want to," He did.

"There are no blank days in the year," he said. "They all have a number and a name and they belong to somebody."

"They do?"

"Yes," he replied. "There are none that don't belong to somebody." He turned to September twenty-third. "I shall call this the first day of autumn," he said. He printed on this date the words "Welcome Fall."

He pulled my card file toward him. "Is my name in your card file?" he asked. "Is there a card with my name on it like the doctor has? Is there one?"

"Why don't you look and see?" I said.

He looked through the cards filed under the initial of his last name. "No. It isn't here," he said. "I'll look under D. Maybe you filed it under D. It should be under my last name, but I'll look for Dibs."

"Check and see," I said. He did. However, his name was not in the card file.

"It isn't there," he said.

"Do you want it to be there?"

"Yes."

"Well, why don't you put it there, then?" I said.

He selected a blank card, carefully printed his name, address, telephone number. Then he filed it correctly under the index heading of the initial of his last name. He took out another blank card, printed my name on it, addressed it "The Playroom," asked the telephone number of the Center, wrote that on the card, filed this one under A.

The church chimes rang again. "It is almost time to eat dinner," he said. He crossed to the window and looked out. He could see the growing crowds of people streaming toward the subway entrance. He watched them. "People going home from work, home from work, home from work," he said. "Going east when they go home from work. Going to their suppers. Then tomorrow they will come again. They will come again west. Come west in the morning and come back to work."

"Yes," I said.

"All the people are going home," he said. "All the work people are going home. Going home to eat their suppers. Going home for the night. All the people are going east. Then, to come to work in the morning, it'll be they come west."

"Yes, that's right. If they come on the subway or the bus," I said. "They are going home now. In the morning they will probably come back to work."

"Yes," said Dibs. "Back and forth. Day after day. Day after day. Gets monotonous."

He stood there, looking quietly out the window for a long time. Then he turned and looked at me. "Where is Mother?"

"She hasn't come yet. They will ring the buzzer and let us know when she is here."

"They will?"

"Yes."

"This you *know* will happen?" he asked.

"Yes. I know it will."

"Some one out there *said* they would buzz it when she came?" he asked.

"Yes. What do you think?"

"They don't always do what they say," he said.

"You feel that sometimes you expect something to happen and you are disappointed?" I asked.

"Yes," he replied. "It can happen. But if you say you believe, there is something else I must do."

"What must you do?" I asked.

He pulled the calendar toward him and leafed through it. He turned to the current day. "This is today," he said. "I will put a big X on it."

"An X on today?" I said. "Why?"

"Because it is my most important day," he said.

"Why is today an important day for you?" I asked.

"It is my most important day," he said quite seriously. "I *know*."

He thumbed idly through the calendar. "This is Easter" he said, indicating the correct date.

"Yes, it is."

"It'll be a pretty day."

"It will?"

"Yes. Easter. Lots of flowers and church. Is that not so?" he asked.

"Yes," I replied.

The buzzer sounded. "Like you said," Dibs remarked, pointing to the door.

"Yes. That's your mother now."

"I know," Dibs said. "Goodbye." He walked up to me, touched my hand shyly. "Goodbye, Miss A," he said.

We walked out to the waiting room together. His mother greeted me in a friendly, relaxed manner. Dibs stood beside her quietly. As they started to leave the outer office, his mother said, "Say goodbye to . . ."

"Goodbye," Dibs interrupted to say, flatly, mechanically.

"He said goodbye to me before we left my office," I told his mother.

Dibs brightened. "Goodbye, again, Miss A," he said. "Happy goodbye."

Chapter Fourteen

I WAS IN THE RECEPTION ROOM when Dibs and his mother arrived the following week. I was wearing a silk print dress.

"Oh look, Mother," Dibs cried. "The pretty colored dress. Aren't those pretty? Isn't the dress pretty?"

"Yes," his mother said. "It is a very pretty dress."

"Colors," Dibs said. "Beautiful colors."

This was quite different from his usual quiet entrance. His mother smiled. "Dibs insisted on bringing one of his birthday gifts to show you," she said. "Is it all right with you?"

"Of course it is," I said. "If he wanted to bring it with him, it's quite all right."

"Well, he wanted to," his mother said.

Dibs was anxious to get back to the playroom. He was carrying a large box, apparently containing the birthday gift.

"He can explain it to you," his mother said. "In fact, I'm beginning to think he has all the answers." There was an unmistakable note of pride in her voice.

Dibs had already gone back to the playroom. I followed him. He sat on the ledge of the sandbox and unwrapped his gift. "I'm here," he announced. "I'm here."

"I see. Well, make yourself at home," I answered.

"Not at home!" Dibs replied. "At playroom!"

"All right," I said. "Make yourself at playroom!"

Dibs strutted around the playroom smiling happily. "I had a birthday," he said.

"Did you have a happy birthday?" I asked.

139

"Yes," Dibs answered. He went back to the package. "See this? It's an international code set with batteries and all. See? These are dots and these are dashes and it sends messages in code. You spell with dots and dashes and it sends messages in code. No letters, just code." As he moved it the batteries fell out. Quickly he replaced them. "It comes apart," he explained. "These batteries don't fit in too well. Hear the little noises it makes when I press the key? That's the message. Isn't it nice?"

"Yes, Dibs. It is very nice."

"It is very, very interesting." He pressed down the key and clicked out a message. "See how it works? It's an international code set and anyone can read it if they know the code."

"I see."

A truck drove up outside the window. "You look at truck, Dibs," he said, reverting to his earlier talking pattern. "You open window, Dibs." He opened the window and looked out. "Oh, truck gone," he said.

"It has gone?"

"Yes. Here come another truck." Another truck drove up and parked. Dibs looked at me and grinned. Perhaps this retreat to baby talk was a relief from the pressure of expectations that the birthday gift suggested to him. "Here is truck." Dibs said. "It moves. It stops. Now it backs. The man comes out. He carries something. Four boxes in a row. He takes something inside. He comes out. He gets four more big boxes. He goes inside."

He leaned on the windowsill and studied the truck. He glanced back over his shoulder at me. "It's a big truck. It's a dirty red color. It is full of boxes. I don't know what he has in the boxes but he has a truck full of them. The man goes in and out of the truck. He carries them into the building. Back and forth. In and out. He carries things."

Two college girls carrying books walked past the window. They looked up at Dibs leaning out the window.

"Hello," one of the girls said to Dibs.

He ignored her.

"I said hello," the girl called out. Dibs continued to ignore her.

"Can't you say hello?" asked the girl. "Can't you talk? What's wrong with you? Cat got your tongue?"

Dibs did not say a word. He stood looking out the window, watching them in silence. When they were out of sight, he spoke. "I watch them go by. I don't talk to them. I don't answer them. There goes the man in the truck. I didn't speak to him. There goes a woman walking down the street. I don't speak to her. I don't say a word to any of them. There goes the truck. *Goodbye truck!*" The truck drove away with a roar of the motor.

"Can't you say hello? Can't you talk?" he said imitating the girl's tone of voice. Dibs closed the window with a bang and turned around facing me with his eyes ablaze with anger. "Don't want to say hello! Won't speak to them!" Dibs shouted. "Will not talk!"

"You watch them and hear them speak to you, but they hurt your feelings and you don't want to talk to them," I said.

"That's right," he said. "People are mean so I don't talk to them. But I speak to the truck. I say goodbye to the truck."

"A truck can't say anything to hurt your feelings, can it?" I said.

"The truck is nice," Dibs said.

He walked over to the sandbox, sat down on the ledge, and raked his fingers through the sand. He pulled out a toy soldier, held it in his hands, and looked at it for a long time. Then he turned toward the sand, dug a hole with his hands, and buried the soldier. On top of the mound of sand he placed a toy truck. Without a word, he made this graphic statement to dramatize his feelings.

Then he collected the little sand bucket, a plastic bowl, a spoon, some cookie pans, and a sifter. These he arranged on the table. "Now I will bake cookies," he announced. "Today is the cook's day off and I'll bake cookies. It'll take my mind off my worries," he said. He began to measure and mix the sand in his bowl. "I'll take flour and sugar and shortening," he said. "I'll get the sifter and sift the flour. Sift it three times. I sift it like this, Dibs, to make it lighter. This will make the cookies taste better. And I'll add the shortening. Butter is sometimes called shortening. So are other things called shortening. Like lard and margarine and vegetable oils." He was engrossed in his role-playing.

"Now I'll add the milk," he said. "Did you notice that I lit the oven so it could be pre-heated? Pre-heated means to warm it up ahead of time. Then I get the cookie-cutters. There are several different shapes. These are rabbits. These are stars. These are pumpkins. Do you have a choice? If you do have a choice, hand it to me. Or push it over to this side of the table. I wish I knew if you understood what I say to you. You understood about the cutters, didn't you? You want me to make rabbit cookies. Now I'll flatten them out with this little rolling pin and I'll cut them with the cookie-cutter you selected."

His cookie mixture did not stay in compact form. He glanced at me. "Real cookies stick better," he said. "But I'll pretend these do and I'll shape them with this rabbit cookie-cutter. I'll have to put them in the pan and shape them, but for real cookies you cut them first."

"I see," I commented.

"Now I'll put them in the pre-heated oven," he said. He placed the tray of sand cookies in the toy oven. "Now I'll sit down and wait for the cookies to bake." He sat down on the ledge of the sandbox and removed his shoelaces from his oxfords. He took off his shoes, then crawled into the sandbox and sang.

Oh cookies bake
While I sit in here.
Oh cookies bake
While I pull off my socks
While I pour sand on my feet
While I count my toes.
One, two, three, four, five.
Five toes on one foot.

Oh, what comes after one?
What did I tell you?
Think. Think. Think.
I'll do it again.
You watch me and hear.
One, two, three, four, five.
What did I say?
You say it now.
One, One, One.
What did I say?
Listen again.
One, two, three, four.
One, One, One.
Listen to me
You stupid child.
One, Two, Two, Two.
Now say it again.
One, two, three, four, five.
Right, Right, Right.
A hot baked cookie for you!

He laughed. "So five toes on one foot and five toes on the other foot make ten toes on two feet," he said. "Can't you learn anything? Or do you know and you just won't answer me?"

"Sometimes you knew the answers only you wouldn't say? Is that the way it was?" I asked.

"I don't know when I knew and when I didn't," Dibs said, verbalizing the confusion that must often have been thrust at him. He lay down in the sand on his back and twisted around until he touched his toes to his lips. "See what I can do?" he said. "I can bend double and nobody ever taught me how." He rolled over in the sand. He stood up and jumped up and down in the sand. He ran over to the table, got the nursing bottle, and went back to the sandbox. He lay down and sucked on the bottle like a small baby. He closed his eyes. "When I was a baby," he said.

I waited, but he did not go on. "When you were a baby, then what?" I asked finally.

"When I was a baby," he said again. Then he suddenly sat up. "No. No. No," he said. He quickly got out of the sandbox. "I am not a baby. I was never a baby!"

"You're not a baby now and don't want to think you ever were?" I said.

He crossed to the easel. "There are eleven different colors of paint on the easel," he said. "The different colors are made out of different ingredients. Did you know that?"

"They are?" I commented.

"Yes." He walked restlessly around the room.

"If you are going to stay out of the sandbox perhaps you had better put your socks and shoes on," I said.

"Yes. My feet are cold. This floor is cold today," he replied.

He put his socks on, handed me his shoes and shoelaces. "If I need your help, you will help," he said. "If I don't need, but just want it, you will help."

"Is that the way it is?" I commented.

"Yes," Dibs replied, nodding his head. "I know." I put the shoelaces in his oxfords and handed them to him.

"Thank you," Dibs said.

"You are welcome," I replied.

Dibs smiled. "You welcomed me!" he cried. He flapped his arms up and down and crowed like a rooster. He laughed. "Happy Dibs," he shouted. "Get going, Dibs. To the water. To the sink." He put on his shoes, tied the laces securely, hopped over to the sink, opened the doors, and turned the water on full force. He got the nursing bottle, took it to the sink, emptied the water that was in it, refilled it. The water splashed out into the room. He turned on the drinking fountain, held his finger partly over the hole and directed a stream of water out into the room. "I make a stream of a splash!" he shouted. He rolled up the sleeves of his shirt. He filled the nursing bottle, tried to put the nipple on, but it was too slippery.

"Miss A will do it for you, Dibs," he said. "Miss A will not turn you down."

"You think I'll fix it for you?"

"That's right," said Dibs. "I know you will." He handed me the bottle and the nipple. I put it on for him, returned the bottle to him.

He stood in front of me sucking on the bottle, looking steadily at me. "You do not call me stupid," he said. "I say help, you help. I say I don't know, you know. I say I can't, you can."

"And how does that make you feel?" I asked.

"Like that," he said. "I *feel*." He looked at me steadily, seriously. He turned back to the sink, filled the bottle, emptied it, turned on the faucet, splashed the water, laughed as he poured water on the drainboard and on the floor. "Make it sloppy wet!" he cried. "Make it a real mess!" He noticed a can of scouring powder on the shelf above the sink. He climbed up and got it.

"What is in this can?" he asked.

"Scouring powder," I said.

He smelled it, shook some out in his hand, looked at it, then suddenly put it in his mouth to taste.

"Oh no, Dibs!" I exclaimed. "That's scouring powder. Not good to taste!"

He turned and looked at me coldly. This sudden reaction of mine was inconsistent. "How can I tell how it tastes unless I taste?" he asked with dignity.

"I don't know of any other way," I told him. "But I don't think you ought to swallow it. It isn't good to taste."

He spit it in the sink.

"Why don't you rinse your mouth out with some water?" I suggested. He did. But my reaction disturbed him. He put the scouring powder back on the shelf and gave me a cold look.

"I'm sorry, Dibs," I said. "I guess I just didn't think. But I didn't like to see you take such a big mouthful of scouring powder."

He bit his lip, walked over to the window. His sensitive

armor was ready to put on quickly when his feelings were hurt. Finally, he went back to the sink. He filled the pitcher with water and poured it on the drainboard. He placed the nursing bottles in the water, then filled the sink and smacked them together. The water was running full force. He laughed as he stirred the bottles around in the water. He dropped one of them and it hit the faucet. "They might break and cut!" he cried. "Are you afraid for me?"

"I think you know how to take care of it," I said, having learned my lesson. He removed the glass bottles and tossed the plastic dishes into the water.

"Down and around they go," he yelled. "Little cups. Little saucers. Little plates. Come splash. Come throw." He threw the water out into the room by the cupful, shouting with glee. "Get back. Get back," he yelled. "Watch out for your dress. Keep back and take warning or you'll get wet."

I retreated to a safe corner and Dibs continued to throw the water.

"I've never made such a wonderful mess in all my life!" he shouted. The sink was filling up, getting closer and closer to the point of overflowing. "Look at that water," he exclaimed. "It'll be like a waterfall. It'll overflow." He stood before the sink, watching it, jumping up and down. He plunged his hands and arms down in the water, put his wet hands up on his face, splashed some water on his face. "Oh wet, wet water, so cool, so fast," he said. He bent over until his face touched the water. Just as the water started to overflow, he quickly turned off the faucet.

"I'll let some water out," he announced. He vigorously stirred the cups and saucers around in the water. He dumped in the tiny plastic knives, forks, spoons. "These little things might go down the drain," he said. He scooped them out. He laid them on the drainboard. "That's enough of that," he said, pulling out the stopper. The water gurgled down the drain. He reached toward the hot water faucet.

"That water is too hot, Dibs," I said. "Use the cold water first."

Dibs re-arranged the forks. He counted them. Quickly, he reached up, turned on the hot water, stuck his finger under it, and jerked it back in a hurry.

"It is hot!" he exclaimed.

"You wanted to find out for yourself. Now you know," I said.

"Yes," Dibs said. "Too hot."

He picked up the nursing bottle on the table, put the nipple in his mouth, and sucked on it. He sat down on the little chair beside the table, quite subdued, drinking from the bottle. "I'm not very old," he said.

"You're not?"

"No. I'm only six."

"Right now you don't feel very old, do you?"

"No." He continued to suck on the bottle, looking at me. Finally, he put it down.

"Miss A lives in this big brick building," he said. "She lives in room seventeen. It is her room. She belongs someplace. And room seventeen is her room. It is my room, too."

"It belongs to both of us, does it?"

Dibs nodded his head. "This is a very nice place to be," he said. "And so is your office. Let's go down to your office. I'll take my message set with me."

We went down to my office. Dibs again sat down in the desk chair. He examined the new desk lamp, turned it on, then opened the box containing his code set. "This sends messages," he said.

"What kind of messages?" I asked.

"Just messages," Dibs said. "This is the code for 'a.' This is the code for 'b.' I'll show you the code for all the letters in the alphabet." He clicked off the code for each letter.

"My arms are chapped," he said. "That's why the skin is rough. I'll have to rub them with grease. Oh, look at this nice little book." He picked up the book. "I see you have a *Little Oxford Dictionary*. I'll look up a word in it. Let's see. Y-e-a-s-t. That spells 'yeast.' I'll look it up and read you the definition." He found the word, read the definition. "That's what you use in bread. I like to look up words in a dictionary. Do you understand the code?" he asked me.

"When I can look at it on the box top," I said.

Having established the fact that I might be able to understand his coded messages, he bent over his paper and wrote in code. Then pulling the telegraph set closer to him, he rapidly tapped out the message. "Hear this. Hear this," he cried. "Do you get the message?"

"I'll have to look at the paper and the box top," I said.

"Okay. You look," he said. "This is an important message."

"I think I have it," I said, after decoding it.

"What's it say?" he demanded.

"It says, 'I am Dibs. I am Dibs. I am Dibs.'"

"That's right!" he cried. "Now get this." He clicked away on the telegraph set.

"I like Dibs. You like Dibs. We both like Dibs," I read the message back to him. He clapped his hands.

"That's right," he cried. "We do!" He smiled happily. "Now you write something and I'll click it off," he said. "Ask me something."

I printed the code, "How old are you?"

"I am six," he wrote for his answer. "I have just had a birthday. I like me. You like me. I will save these messages."

He folded the paper upon which we had written our code and filed it in the index card file behind his card. "Everything under A belongs to you. Everything under my card belongs to me. I'm going to take everything else out of here. One card for you. One card for me. Just our two cards in this box together. And no others."

"You just want your card and my card in the box?" I asked.

"Yes. Just us two. No one else."

He put the lid on his signal set. "This is a nice set," he

said. "It was a birthday present. Mother gave it to me. Papa gave me a chemistry set. Dorothy gave me a book. And Grandma gave me a big, beautiful musical top. She sent it to me in the mail. And some jellybeans and some balloons in a box." He laughed. "She sent me a teddy bear last year. He's my real pet."

"You are fond of your teddy bear, are you? You seem to like all the presents you got for your birthday," I commented.

"I do," he said. "And the birthday card, too. I liked the card you sent me. I liked my birthday this year."

"I'm glad you did," I said.

"It's almost time to go, isn't it?" he said, turning the desk clock toward him.

"Yes."

"I'll have three minutes of just this," he said, folding his hands on the desk in front of him, watching the hands of the clock. "I'm being happy," he said.

When the time was up he picked up his code set and started out the door. "Goodbye, Miss A," he said.

"Goodbye, Dibs."

"You stay in here," he said. "I'll come back next week."

Chapter Fifteen

"GOOD AFTERNOON," Dibs called out as he came into the playroom. "Another day brings me back to the magic room where I do whatever it is I have to do. Today I have planned the things I must do."

"You have plans for today?" I remarked. "Well, whatever you decide to do is up to you."

He walked around the playroom looking at the sandbox, studying the doll house, picking up each member of the doll family. "I see Papa is here," he said. "And Mother. And there are the sister and the boy. They are all here in the house." He replaced them and walked over to the window and looked out for a long time in silence.

"The family is there in the house," I commented; then I joined him in silence as he stood gazing out the window.

Finally, he sighed deeply. He half turned and glanced back at me. "There are so many things in the world," he said. "Just looking out this window I can see so many wonderful things. Trees that grow so big and strong. And a church that reaches up to the sky. I see people walking by. There are all kinds of people. I see some cars and trucks. And these people. There are all kinds of people. Sometimes I am afraid of people."

"Sometimes you are afraid of people?" I said, hoping he would be encouraged to go on.

"But sometimes I'm not afraid of people," he added. "I'm not afraid of you."

"You don't feel afraid when you're with me?" I commented.

"No," he said. He sighed. "I'm not afraid now when I'm with you."

He walked over to the sandbox and sifted the sand through his fingers. "Sand is useful for so many things," he said. He took the shovel and started to dig a deep hole. "Somebody might get buried in this hole," he said. "They just might."

"Oh. Might someone get buried there?"

"Then again they might not," he added, backing away from the idea.

"You haven't made up your mind just yet?" I said.

He walked away from the sandbox, crossed over to the table, and idly handled the crayons. "I am a boy," he said slowly. "I have a father, a mother, a sister. But I do have a grandmother and she loves me. Grandmother has always loved me. But not Papa. Papa has not always loved me."

"You feel sure of Grandmother's love, but not so sure Papa has always loved you?" I remarked.

Dibs twisted his hands together. "Papa likes me some better now," he said. "Papa talks to me."

"You feel Papa likes you better now?" I remarked. I felt this was a very delicate situation; and prodding would cause Dibs to scurry away into the underbrush of his impassive silent defense.

"Some little better," Dibs said. He twisted his hands together as though he felt agitated.

"I have a microscope," he said. "I look at many interesting things under the microscope. Then I can see them bigger than they are and I know them better. Some things you can see under a microscope that are not there without it."

Dibs was off again into the safe world of his intellectualism. The microscope was a thing. There was no need to fear this object. There were no feelings tangled up with it.

"There are times when you find the microscope interesting," I said. Then I waited.

Dibs picked up a crayon. He made idle, meaningless

marks on the paper. "In here I am safe," he said. "You won't let anything hurt me."

"You feel safe in here with me," I remarked. He was leading up to something of importance to him. I had to proceed with utmost caution so that I would not get in his way or push him ahead before he was ready.

He went over to the doll house and took the dolls out.

He arranged the furniture.

"The mother is going for a walk in the park," he said. "She wants to be alone and so she goes walking in the park where she can see the trees and flowers and birds. She even goes over to the lake and watches the water." He moved the mother doll away through his imagined park. "She finds a bench and sits down to feel the sun because she likes the sun." He placed the mother doll on a block and returned to the house. He picked up the sister doll. "The sister is going away to school. They have packed the bags and sent her away from home and she goes far away all by herself." He removed the sister doll to a far corner of the playroom. Then he returned to the doll house and picked up the father doll.

"He is in the house alone. He is reading and studying and he must not be disturbed. He is all alone. He does not want to be bothered. He lights his pipe and he smokes because he can't decide what to do. Then he goes over and unlocks the little boy's room." He quickly put down the father doll and picked up the little boy doll. "The boy opens the door and runs out of the house because he doesn't like the locked doors." He moved the boy doll, but not too far away from the house.

Dibs buried his face in his hands and was very quiet while the minutes ticked away. He sighed deeply and picked up the father doll. "So Papa goes out for a walk, too, because he doesn't know what to do. He walks down the street and there are lots of cars and buses and traffic going by making such a big noise and Papa doesn't like noise. But he is going down the street to the toy store and he is going to buy some wonderful new toys for his boy."

He thinks maybe the boy would like a microscope. So he buys it and goes back to the house."

Dibs got up and paced the room, glancing at me from time to time. Then he knelt down beside the house again and picked up the father doll. "He called and called to the boy and the boy came running in." Dibs brought the boy doll back beside the father. "But the boy ran in so fast he bumped into the table and upset the lamp. The father cried out that the boy was stupid. A stupid, silly, careless boy! 'Why did you do that?' he demanded, but the boy wouldn't answer him. The father was very angry and told the boy to go to his room. He said he was a stupid, silly child and he was ashamed of him."

Dibs was tensed up, immersed in this scene he was playing out. He looked up at me and must have felt that I was as deeply in the experience as he was. "The boy slipped out of the house and hid," Dibs whispered. "The father didn't notice what happened. Then. . . ." He got up and hurried across the room after the mother doll and brought her back to the house. "The mother was finished with her park visit and so she came back. The father was still very angry and he told the mother what the stupid boy had done. And the mother said 'Oh dear! Oh dear! What is the matter with him?' Then all of a sudden a boy giant came along. He was so big nobody could ever hurt him." Dibs stood up. "This giant boy saw the mother and father in the house and he heard what angry things they said. So he decided to teach them a lesson. He went all around the house and he locked every window and every door so they could not get out. They were both locked in."

He looked up at me. His face was pale and grim. "You see what is happening?" he said.

"Yes. I see what is happening. The father and mother are locked in the house by the giant boy."

"Then the father says he is going to smoke his pipe and he gets it out and gets some matches and he strikes a match and drops it on the floor and the room catches on fire. The house is on fire! The house is on fire! And they cannot get out. They are locked in the house and the fire is burning faster and faster. The little boy sees them in the house where they are locked in and burning and he says 'Let them burn! Let them burn!'" Dibs made quick, darting snatches at the mother and father doll as though he would save them, but he drew back and shielded his face as though the fire he imagined was very real and burning him as he attempted to save the father and mother.

"They scream and cry and beat on the door. They want to get out. But the house is burning and they are locked in and they can't get out. They scream and cry for help."

Dibs clasped his hands together and tears streamed down his face. "I weep! I weep! I weep!" he cried to me. "Because of this I weep!"

"Do you weep because the mother and father are locked in the house and can't get out and the house is burning?" I asked.

"Oh no!" Dibs replied. A sob caught his voice and broke it. He stumbled across the room to me and flung his arms around my neck while he wept bitter tears.

"I weep because I feel again the hurt of doors closed and locked against me," he sobbed. I put my arm around him.

"You are feeling again the way you used to feel when you were so alone?" I said.

Dibs glanced back at the doll house. He brushed away his tears and stood there breathing heavily. "The boy will save them," he said. He went to the boy doll and took him to the house. "I'll save you! I'll save you!" he cried. "I'll unlock the doors and let you out. And so the little boy unlocked the doors and put the fire out and his father and mother were safe."

He came back to me and touched my hand. He smiled wanly. "I saved them," he said. "I didn't let them get all burned up and hurt."

"You helped them. You saved them," I said.

Dibs sat down at the table, staring straight ahead.

"They used to lock me in my room," he said. "They don't do it any more, but they used to."

"They did? But not any more?"

"Not any more," Dibs said, and a trembling sigh escaped him. "Papa really did give me a microscope and I have lots of fun with it." He got up from the table and went across the playroom to the spot where he had put the sister doll. He carried her back to the doll house and put all four dolls in chairs in the living room.

Then he went back to the table and picked up the black crayon and colored a piece of drawing paper a solid black except for a tiny circle in the middle of the paper. This circle he colored yellow. He made no comment about his drawing. When he was finished he put the crayons back in the box. Then he went over to the sandbox, picked up the shovel, and slowly filled in the hole that he had dug earlier in the hour.

It had been a rough hour for Dibs. His feelings had torn through him without mercy. The locked doors in Dibs' young life had brought him intense suffering. Not the locked door of his room at home, but all the doors of acceptance that had been closed and locked against him, depriving him of the love, respect, and understanding he needed so desperately.

Dibs picked up the nursing bottle and drank from it briefly. Then he put it down and looked steadily at me. "I'm not a baby any more," he said. "I'm a big boy now. I don't need the baby bottle."

"You don't need the baby bottle any more?" I commented.

Dibs grinned. "Unless I sometimes want to be a baby again," he said. "However I feel, I feel. However I feel, I will be."

He spread wide his arms in an expansive gesture. "Cock-a-doodle-do," he crowed. "Cock-a-doodle-do!"

He was relaxed and happy now. When he left the playroom he seemed to leave behind him the sorrowful feelings he had uprooted there.

Chapter Sixteen

When Dibs came into the playroom he smiled happily as he looked about him. He noticed a stretch of fence that another child had built across the middle of the sandbox. "There is a fence," he said. "And you know I don't like fences. I'll take it out of there." Quickly, he removed the fence from the sandbox. Then he picked up the gun and carried it over to the table where he placed it in the drawer. He noticed a small broken doll house on the shelf, picked it up, examined it.

"I'll fix this," he said. "Where's some Scotch Tape?"

I got out some Scotch Tape. "How much do you think you'll need?" I asked.

"Ten inches," he said quickly, which was about the amount he did need.

I tore off about ten inches of tape and handed it to him.

"This is fine," Dibs said. "Thank you."

"You're welcome," I replied.

"Well! You are welcome, too," Dibs exclaimed. "And now I will open the window so fresh air can come in." He opened the window. "Come in, air," he cried out. "Come on in and be with us." He grinned at me. "Papa doesn't like me to talk to the air, but in here I will if I feel like it."

"In here, if you feel like it, okay," I remarked.

"Papa says people just talk to people," Dibs said. "There was a twinkle in his eye. "Papa says I ought to talk to him, but I don't. I listen to him, but I don't talk to him.

No, often I do not answer him. It upsets him very much."

Talking had became an issue between the two of them and Dibs was an expert at withholding speech as a way of getting back at his critical father.

"'Good morning,' he said to me," Dibs continued. "I don't look at him. I don't answer him. 'What is the matter with you?' he says. 'I know you can talk.' But I don't say anything. I don't look at him. I don't answer." Dibs laughed. "He gets so upset!"

He went back to the table, opened the drawer, and took out the gun. Then he crossed over to the open window and looked out. He watched a big truck go by.

He turned and looked at me. "Throw this gun out?" he asked.

"If you did we couldn't get it again," I said.

"I would be right down there below the window," he said.

"I know. But we couldn't go out and get it now."

"Later it might be gone," Dibs said. "Someone might find it and take it away."

"Yes. That is possible."

"Well, then I'll not throw it out," Dibs said.

He walked around the doll house and looked at the family of dolls. He stood up the father doll and aimed the gun at him. "Don't you say a word or I'll shoot you," he said to the doll. "Don't you open your mouth once more." He clicked the gun. "I'm getting ready. If you are not careful, I'll shoot you."

He opened the lower part of the house. "I'll hide the gun down here in the basement," he said. "Nobody is going to get hurt." He put the gun in the lower part of the house and closed the door.

Then he came over and stood in front of me, a little smile lighting up his face. "There are children in my room at school," he said, after a long pause. "There is Jack and John and David and Carl and Bobby and Jeffrey and Jane and Carol. There are lots of children in my room at school."

"Lots of children at school with you? You know the names of some of them, don't you?"

"I know the names of all of them," Dibs said. "There are boys and girls. They are very interesting."

This was the first mention of specific boys and girls in his group at school. It was the first expression of interest in them.

I had thought that at some point along the way we might have some group therapy for Dibs to give him the opportunity to become a part of a small, interacting group. I had had no word from the school and had no way of knowing what progress, if any, he was making there. I decided to ask Dibs what he thought of the idea of bringing another child here in the playroom with him.

"Dibs, would you like to have another little boy or girl come here and play with you on Thursdays?" I asked.

Dibs seemed almost to jump. He looked at me directly with angry eyes. "No! No!" he shouted. "Don't want anybody else in here!"

"You don't want another child in here with you?" I asked.

Dibs seemed to slump. "Nobody else would come," he said sadly.

"You don't think anyone else would come? Is that why you said no?"

"No," Dibs mumbled. "Nobody likes me. Nobody would come."

"But if another child would come and wanted to come and be with you, would that make a difference?" I asked, pushing the idea at him tentatively.

"No!" shouted Dibs. "This is mine! I want it all mine! I don't want anybody else to ever come here. I want this just for me and for you." He seemed close to tears. He turned his back to me.

"I understand, Dibs," I said. "If you want this to be just for you and me, then that's the way it will be."

"It'll be that way," Dibs said. "I want this just all mine with nobody else ever coming in here."

"Whatever way you want it," I said.

Dibs walked over to the window and looked out. Silence fell over both of us.

"There are children in my room at school," he said, after a long silence. "I. . . ." He hesitated, turned and looked at me. "I . . . like . . . them," he said, stammering a little. "I want them to like me. But I don't want them in here with us. You are just for me. Something special just for me. Just us two."

"You like the other children, but you want to keep this time just for the two of us?"

"Yes. That's right." The chimes rang. "Four o'clock," he said. "Four o'clock chimes and four o'clock flowers. And the sun is in the sky. And there are sunflowers. There are so many different things."

"Yes," I said.

He went over to the sink and turned the water on full force. Then he turned it to a tiny stream. He looked at me and said, quite seriously, "I can make the water trickle and gush. The way *I* want it to be."

"Yes. You can manage the water in here the way you want it."

"I can stop it. I can go it," he said.

"You can control it," I remarked.

"Yes," he said, slowly and deliberately. "I can. I. I. I. . . ." He walked around the playroom, patting his chest, calling out, "I. I. I. I." He stopped in front of me. "I am Dibs," he said. "I can do things. I like Dibs. I like me." He smiled happily, then started to play in the water.

He put the nursing bottle in the sink and turned the water on full force. It splashed all over the playroom. He jumped back and laughed heartily. "It doesn't splash me!" he cried. "I can jump back out of its way. I can do something about it." He put a small bottle into a larger bottle. He held one bottle high in the air and poured the water down into the smaller bottle. "Oh, I can do things," he exclaimed. "I can do this and this and this. I can make experiments." With the water and the various containers, he conducted his experiments. "This is fun," he cried. "Things together do funny things. I can be as big as all

the world in here. I can do anything I want to do. I am
big and powerful. I can make the water come and go.
Anything I want to do, I can do. Hello, there, little bottle.
How are you? Are you having fun? Don't talk to the little
bottle. The little bottle is only a thing. Talk to people.
Talk to people, I say. Hello, John. Hello, Bobby. Hello,
Carl. Talk to people. But I want to say hello to the little
bottle and if I want to, in here, I can."

Quickly he picked out the nursing bottle and the nipple. "Put this on for me," he asked. I did, while he held
the bottle.

He drank from the bottle and stood looking at me while
he did. "When I want to be a baby, I can be. When I
want to be grown-up, I can be. When I want to talk, I
talk. When I want to be still, I be still. Isn't that so?"

"Yes. That's the way it is," I said.

He removed the nipple and drank from the bottle. "Let
me show you something interesting," he said. He got out
some glasses, lined them up, and then poured different
amounts of water in each glass. He picked up a spoon and
tapped each glass. "Hear the different sounds?" he cried
out. "I can make each glass sound different. The amount
of water in the glass makes the difference. Listen when I
hit the pipe. And this tin box. Every sound is different.
And there are some sounds I don't make, but they happen. Thunder is a sound. And dropping things makes
noise. The bottle makes a noise. Yes. I can make all kinds
of sounds. And I can be so quiet. I can make no noise at
all. I can make silence."

"You can make sounds and silence," I said.

He had had his hands in the water for a long time. He
held them out to me. "Look. My hands are all wrin-
kled."

"I see."

"Now I have something very important to do," he said.
He placed the jars of paint on the ledge of the easel in a
haphazard fashion. "Look at that," he said. "Red, blue,
yellow, grey, orange, violet, green, white. All mixed up.
And I've just put the wrong brush in every color." He did

just that. He stood back and looked at the easel and laughed. "Any old way," he said. "That's the way they are. All mixed up. And the wrong brush in the wrong jar. That's the way I did it. I did it all wrong." He laughed.

"So you mixed them all up—paints and brushes," I said.

"Yes," he said. "A great big mess. A mess of a mix-up. Probably the first real mess I ever made. But now I must put them in their proper order and take the brushes out and do it correctly." He started to re-arrange the paints and straighten up the mess.

"Do you feel that you must put them in a certain order?" I asked.

"Oh yes," he said. "There are twelve brushes and twelve colors." He laughed.

"Oh come, Dibs, fix them right," he said, lightly. "There is a correct way to do everything and you get them all in their proper order."

"Do you think they should always be in a certain order?" I asked.

"Oh yes," he said, with a grin. "That is unless they all are mixed up."

"Then either way is all right?"

"In here," he said. "Remember, in here, it's all right just to be."

He came over to me and patted my hand. "You understand," he said, with a smile. "Let's go down to your office. Let's go visiting you in your office."

"We can go down there for the rest of the time if you want to," I said.

He went eagerly down the hall to my office. There was a package of bookplates on the desk. He picked them up. "May I open them and use them?" he asked.

"If you want to."

He went over to the bookshelves and studied the books carefully. He selected one and read the title, "Your child meets the world outside." He went over to the window and looked out. "Hello, world," he said. "Well, it's a beautiful day for the world outside. It smells good outside, too. Ah, here comes my friendly truck."

He watched in silence for a long time.

"Hello, truck," he said, softly. "Hello, man. Hello, world." He smiled happily.

Then he came back to the desk and picked up the *Little Oxford Dictionary*. "Little old book full of words," he said. "I'll put two in here. My little dictionary. Blue-backed book of words." He pasted two bookplates in the book. Then he leaned back in the desk chair and looked at me. There was a big smile on his face. "Soon it'll be time to go home," he said. "And when I go, I'll be all happy inside. Then I'll come back again next Thursday. And remember, only me. Nobody else, but me. And you."

"I'll remember," I said. "If you want this time just for you, that's quite all right with me."

"I want it for us," Dibs whispered. "But not yet anybody else."

"Then that's the way it will be," I said, "not yet anybody else."

I wondered if perhaps a seed had been sowed and he might suggest that he would like to bring a friend. Or if not in here, perhaps he would have a friend at school.

The buzzer sounded signaling the arrival of his mother.

"Goodbye," he said. "I'll be back next Thursday and fill up again with happiness."

When he stepped outside, in his mother's presence, he looked up at me. "Goodbye, again," he said. Then he turned and ran down the long hall as fast as he could run, turned, ran back, and flung his arms around his mother. "Oh, mother, I love you!" he cried out as he hugged her.

Both of us were surprised at this spontaneous expression from Dibs. His mother's eyes filled with sudden tears. She nodded her farewell and left, clutching his hand tightly in hers.

Chapter Seventeen

THE NEXT DAY Dibs' mother called for an appointment. I was glad to see her the same day. She came into my office with a restrained eagerness. The spontaneous expression of Dibs' affection on the day before had taken her out of her tight defensiveness.

"I wanted you to know how grateful we are," she said. "Dibs has changed so much. He isn't the same child. I've never before seen him express such free feeling as he did yesterday when we were leaving. I—I was deeply touched."

"I know you were," I commented.

"He is so much better," she said. There was a happy glow in her eyes, a little smile on her lips. "He is calmer and happier. He doesn't have temper tantrums any more. He hardly ever sucks his thumb. He looks directly at us. He answers us when we speak to him most of the time. He shows an interest in what is going on in the family. Sometimes he plays with his sister when she is home. Not always, but sometimes he will. He is beginning to show some affection to me. He will come up to me sometimes and make a comment about something on his own. The other day he came into the kitchen where I was making some cookies and he said 'I see you're busy making cookies. Your cookies are very good to eat. You make the cookies for us.' *Us.* I think he is beginning to feel that he belongs to the family now. And I think ... well, I think I am beginning to feel that he is one of us.

"I don't know what went wrong between us. From the beginning I was at such a loss with him. I felt so completely defeated and threatened. Dibs had ruined everything for me. He threatened my marriage. He ended my career. Now I ask myself what I have done to cause this problem between us? Why did this all happen? What can I do now to help set things right? I've asked myself again and again, why? Why? Why? Why did we fight each other so? So much so that it almost destroyed Dibs. I remember when I first talked to you that I insisted that Dibs was mentally retarded. But I knew he wasn't really retarded. I had been teaching him and testing him and trying to force him to behave in a normal fashion ever since he was two years old—all of it without any real contact between the two of us. Always going through *things*. I don't know what he does here in the playroom. I don't know if you see any sign of all the things he knows and can do. He can read. Almost anything he picks up. He can write and spell—meaningfully. He keeps records of things he is interested in. He has scrapbooks he has made of all different kinds of bark and leaves. He has pressed flowers. He has a room full of books, pictures, things from which he can learn, educational games, toys, science materials. A record player. A vast collection of records. He loves music —especially the classics. He can identify almost any part of any one of them. I know this because now he will say what it is when I play a part and ask him. I'll put a record on, stop it after playing a brief part of it, ask him what it is and now he will call out the name. Many hours I spent, playing those records for him, telling him what they were —and never really knowing if I was getting through to him. I have read hundreds of books to him—while he hid under a table. I have talked to him constantly, explaining everything around him. Over and over and over again, encouraged only by the fact that he kept close enough to listen and he looked at the things I showed him."

She sighed and shook her head despairingly. "I had to prove something to myself," she said. "I had to prove that he could learn. I had to prove that *I* could teach him. And yet his behavior was such that I never knew how much got through to him or how much it all meant. I would watch him bend over the things I had given him when he was alone in his own room and I would say to myself, 'He wouldn't do this if it meant nothing to him.' And yet I was never sure."

"You must have been extremely disturbed and ambivalent in your feelings about him," I remarked. "Testing, observing, doubting yourself and Dibs. Hoping and despairing, feeling such a failure and wanting to make it up to him somehow."

"Yes," she said. "Always testing him. Always doubting his capacity. Trying to get closer to him and all the time only building a wall between us. And he always did just enough to keep me at it. I don't think any child was ever so tormented with the constant demands made upon him that he pass this test and that test—always, always he had to prove that he had capacity. He had no peace. Except when his grandmother came to visit. They had a good relationship with each other. He relaxed with her. He didn't talk much to her. But she accepted him the way he was and she always believed in him. She used to tell me that if I relaxed and let him alone he'd come out of it all right. But I couldn't believe that. I felt that I had to make up to him for all the other deficiencies I had given him. I felt responsible for the way he was. I felt guilty."

Suddenly she was in tears. "I don't know how I could have done this to him," she cried. "My intelligence seemed to have flown out the window. My behavior was compulsive and completely unreasonable. I could see the proof I wanted to see that down under that peculiar behavior there was ability. And I couldn't bear to admit to myself that I had done anything that had caused his problems. I couldn't admit that I rejected him. I can only say this now because I no longer reject him. Dibs is my child and I am proud of him." She looked at me searchingly.

"It has been extremely difficult for you to admit your feelings toward Dibs. But now your feelings have changed and you accept him and believe in him and are proud of him?" I commented.

She nodded vigorously. "Let me show you something else he can do. He can read, write, spell, study things.

And his drawings are quite unique. Let me show you some of his drawings."

She suddenly held a roll of papers that she had brought with her. She took off the rubber band, unrolled them, then handed them to me. "Look at them," she said. "Look at the detail and the perspective."

I looked at the drawings. They were indeed unusual for a child of six to have produced. The objects he had drawn were precise down to the last detail. In one picture, he had drawn a park with winding rock steps winding up the hill. The perspective was quite remarkable. "Yes. They are unusual," I said.

She spread them out before her and studied them. Then she looked at me with troubled eyes. "Too unusual," she said, quietly. "That is what worries me with all this strange ability. I've tortured myself with the thought that he might be schizophrenic. And if that is true, what is the value of this superior and unnatural ability? But now I feel free of that fear. He's beginning to behave in a more normal manner."

This mother had studied medicine and she knew that her diagnosis could have been correct. The abnormal behavior she had thrust upon Dibs had kept him apart from his family and from the other children and adults he had met at school. When a child is forced to prove himself as capable, results are often disastrous. A child needs love, acceptance and understanding. He is devastated when confronted with rejection, doubts, and never-ending testing.

"I'm still confused about so many things," she said. "If Dibs has superior ability, it should not be wasted. His accomplishments are something to be proud of."

"All these accomplishments mean a lot to you even though you are still confused about his total development, aren't you?" I said.

"Yes," she replied. "His accomplishments are very important. To him as well as to me. I remember when he was two years old. That's when he learned to read. His father said I was out of my mind when I told him Dibs could read. He said no two-year-old could learn to read, but I knew he could. I had taught him to read."

"How did he learn to read?" I asked.

"I got him two sets of the alphabet. Letters that are cut out. And I showed him each letter, told him what it was and what the sound of the letter was. Then I lined them up in order and he sat there looking at them. Then I took them down and told him to do it just the way I had done it. But he ran out of the room. I put them up in order again and put the other box of letters beside them. Then I walked away and he came back and looked at them. Then I took the other letters and matched them up showing him the right side up and saying what each letter was. Then I took the second set down and asked him to match them up. Again he ran out of the room and I walked away, knowing that he would come back and look at them if I left him alone. Then I did the same thing again. The third time, when I left him alone, he matched up the letters. And very soon he could set up the letters in order by himself.

"Then I got pictures of all kinds of things and told him what each picture showed and printed the word and explained it to him. Then I spelled out the words with the cut-out letters. Soon Dibs was doing this, spelling out a word and putting the correct picture by it. Well, that is reading. Then I got him many books with pictures and words. I got him little storybooks and read them to him again and again. I got him records of singing games, stories, poems. I was always trying new things. He learned to operate his record player. He learned to read the titles of his records. I'd say 'Get me the record about the little train.' He would go through his records and come back with the right one and put it on the coffee table in front of me. And he would always be right. I'd say 'Bring me the word that says tree.' He would bring it to me. Any word I asked for. After a while his father agreed that he seemed to be reading. He would pore over his books. Then sometimes his father would read to him. He would bring things home and explain in detail what the objects were. Then he would leave them for Dibs to examine later when he came to take them into his room. Then I started with numbers and he quickly learned that. He muttered a lot and I felt that he was talking to himself. But there was never any real contacts between us. That's why I worried so about him."

Her voice trailed off into silence. She looked out the window for a long time. I made no comment. The picture she had painted of her life with Dibs had a chill in it. It was, indeed, a wonder that the child had maintained his integration and receptiveness. The pressure he had endured was enough to drive any child into a protective withdrawal. She had proved to herself that Dibs could learn the tasks she set before him. But she had felt the absence of a close relationship with her son. This kind of exploitation of the child's ability, to the exclusion of a balanced emotional life, could destroy him.

"We sent his sister away to school—my aunt's school— so I could concentrate on Dibs," she said in a low voice. "I'm asking myself why, even now, I think all these accomplishments are so important. He was a baby when I started to drive him to prove himself to me. Why can't I let Dibs just be a child? *My* child! And be glad for him. I remember telling you that he rejected me. Why? Why do I reject my own feelings? Why am I afraid to be an emotional person? Why have I taken out on Dibs the strained relationship that grew up between my husband and myself? Because that is what happened. I thought the role of a mother wouldn't interest or hold a man of such brilliance. And he had never wanted children. We fought every indication that we were at fault. Guilt, defeat, frustration, failure. Those were our feelings and we couldn't tolerate them. We blamed Dibs. Poor little Dibs. Everything that went wrong between us was his fault. Everything was his fault. I wonder if we can ever make it up to him."

"There have been many intense, troubled feelings tangled up in this relationship," I said. "You have named some of them. You have talked about your feelings in the past. What are your feelings now?"

"My feelings have changed," she said, slowly. "My feelings are changing. I am proud of Dibs. I love him. Now he doesn't have to prove himself to me every minute. Because he has changed. He had to change first. He had to be bigger than I. And his father's feelings and attitudes have changed. We had built up such high walls around ourselves—all of us. Not only Dibs. I had. So had my husband. And if these walls all come down—and they are coming down, then we'll all be a lot happier and closer."

"Attitudes and feelings do change," I said. "I guess you have experienced that."

"Yes. Thank God I have," she replied.

Probably because she had been accepted as she was and felt unthreatened as a mother, she had been able to dig deeply into her own feelings and come up with significant insight and understanding.

So many times a child is not accepted for therapy if the parents refuse to participate and get help for themselves. No one knows how many children are turned away because of this factor. Many times it is more helpful if the parents do come in and work out their share of the problems in the relationship. But it is also true that parents can agree to therapy and be so resistive that little is accomplished. If they are not ready for such an experience, they can seldom profit from it. The defensiveness of a threatened person can be insurmountable. Fortunately for Dibs, his parents were sufficiently sensitive to their child that they, too, changed in understanding and appreciation of his growth. Not only was Dibs finding himself but so were his parents.

Chapter Eighteen

WHEN MISS JANE CALLED ME on Monday, I felt a surge of eagerness to hear what she had to say about Dibs' behavior in school. Surely some of the behavior I had observed in the playroom was spilling over at school. She did not keep me long in suspense.

"I'm happy to report that we see a big change in Dibs," she said. "It has been a gradual change, but we are delighted with Dibs. He will answer us now. Sometimes he will even initiate a conversation. He is happy, calm, and showing an interest in the other children. He speaks very well most of the time, but when something bothers him he lapses back into his abbreviated, immature speech. He refers to himself as 'I' most of the time. Hedda is beside herself with joy. We are all very pleased with him. We thought you would like to know."

"I certainly am glad to know this," I said. "Could we arrange some kind of get-together so I could hear more of the details about the changes in his behavior? Could you and Hedda and I have lunch together someday soon?"

"We'd like that very much," Miss Jane said. "And I know Hedda would. She's been moved up into his group because we thought she would be better with Dibs. She certainly wanted to be with him. And she has helped him a lot."

We had lunch together the following day, and it was a very revealing discussion that we had about Dibs.

He had been slowly, tentatively emerging from his self-imposed isolation. None of us doubted that Dibs had been aware of everything going on around him. Our surmises

were correct—he had been listening and learning as he
crouched on the edge of the group under a table or sat
with his back to the group in apparent detachment. Gradually, he had approached the group more directly. At first
there were brief answers to questions directed to him.
Then he began to do what the other children did. When
he came into the room in the morning, he returned greetings. He carefully took off his coat and hat and hung them
on his own peg in the coat room. He edged up to the other
children gradually, moving his chair closer and closer to
the group for the stories, the music, the conversation.
Occasionally, he replied to a question. With great skill
the teachers conducted the group in such a way that there
was no sudden focus of attention upon Dibs for participa-
tion or talk. But the opportunity for him to take part was
always there.

"He hasn't had a temper tantrum for so long we've
forgotten he had them," Hedda said. "He smiles at the
other children and at us. When he first began to be a
member of our group, he moved closer to me, took my
hand, talked very briefly to me. I was careful to accept
only as much as he wanted to give; I never pushed him. I
made it a point to acknowledge in a friendly way everything he did and said to encourage him to do more. And
then, of course, the other children were so busy going
about their own business that they accepted whatever Dibs
did without question. Gradually Dibs started to follow
directions and he was able to produce whatever instructions called for in a superior way. Then he would go over
to the easel and paint. That was the first thing he did. He
would concentrate on his work as though he were produc-
ing a masterpiece."

Hedda laughed and produced a roll of his paintings
which she spread out. "He's no artist," she said. "But at
least, he's doing something."

I looked at the paintings. They were very simple, typical, six-year-old drawings. The primitive house. The trees.
The flowers. The colors were clear and bright. But why
did Dibs paint such pictures when he was capable of far

more complex art? These could be the paintings of any child of his age—but an odd contribution from a child whose "at home" drawings and paintings were so far beyond his age ability.

"I've brought some of his other work, too," Hedda said. "Here are some stories he wrote. He knows the alphabet and can print and spell a few words." She passed these papers over to me. Dibs had printed laboriously:

> I see a cat.
> I see a dog.
> I see you.

"We have picture cards around the room with the words printed under the objects and the children refer to these for help with spelling. And when a child wants to write a story, we help him. Some of our children are beginning to read. A few of them read quite well. And Dibs is beginning to participate now in reading."

I looked at the words Dibs had printed so clumsily. Mixed feelings struggled within me. Those simple little paintings. Those simple little sentences. Why was Dibs undercutting his ability? Or were these signs of Dibs' adjustment to a group of his own age?

"And he reads, too!" Hedda said, enthusiastically. "He has joined a reading group. He will sit there with the other children, struggling for the words. And when it's his turn he will read the words slowly, not sure of himself, but usually correctly. I really thought that he was able to read better than he does, but he reads as well as any other child in his group and he is trying."

I was baffled by this report. It could mean several things. Certainly the enthusiasm of his teachers was important for Dibs. If I told them that he could do far better than this, they might feel discouraged and dissatisfied with his progress. Dibs had lived in two worlds for too long a time for any of us to expect immediate and complete integration.

Dibs' social progress was the most important factor in

his development now. There was no question about his ability—unless one wanted to raise the question of wasted ability. But at this stage of the game, wasn't personal and social adjustment more important to Dibs than a display of his ability to read, write, or draw in a way that surpassed any other child in his group? What advantage is there in high intellectual achievement if it cannot be used constructively for the good of the individual and the good of others?

"So you think Dibs is making progress in his group," I said—and the remark sounded feeble and inadequate to me.

"He loves music," Miss Jane said. "He is always the first one up in the group. He knows all the songs. He participates in the rhythm band."

"You should see him dance," Hedda said. "He offers to be an elephant or a monkey, or the wind. All by himself. He is clumsy when he first starts, but when he gets involved he moves with grace and rhythm. We don't push him into anything. We are glad for every little step he takes and we feel that he enjoys being a member of the group. And I believe that his mother's attitudes toward Dibs have changed tremendously. When she brings him or comes for him she has a more accepting, pleasant, happy attitude toward Dibs. He takes her hand and goes with her quite willingly. He is a very interesting child!"

"Yes. He is a very interesting child," I remarked. "He seems to be trying with all his might to be an individual and a member of his group."

"The most noticeable change came when he had his birthday. We always celebrate each child's birthday. We have a birthday cake. We gather in a circle, tell a story, then bring out the cake with the lighted candles. The children sing 'Happy Birthday' and the birthday child stands beside me and the cake, then blows out the candles. The cake is cut and passed around to all the children.

"Well, the day we announced that it was Dibs' birthday we didn't know what he would do. In the past, he never participated, although we celebrated his birthday just as we would any other child's. When it was time to come up in the circle, Dibs was there beside me. And when we sang 'Happy Birthday,' Dibs sang louder than any other child there. He sang 'Happy Birthday, Dear Dibs, Happy Birthday to me!' Then after the cake was cut, he passed it around piece by piece with a big smile on his face. He kept saying 'It is my birthday. It is my birthday. Today I am six years old.' "

The teachers were pleased with Dibs. So was I. But we had farther to go. Dibs should learn to accept himself as he was and use his abilities, not deny them. But socially and emotionally, Dibs was achieving new horizons for himself. They were fundamental to his total development. I felt confident that the ability Dibs used in the playroom and at home would spill out into his other experiences. His intellectual abilities had been used to test him. They had become a barrier and a refuge from a world he feared. It had been defensive, self-protective behavior. It had been his isolation. And if Dibs did begin to talk, read, write, draw, in ways far beyond those of the other children around him, he would be avoided by them and isolated for his differences.

There are far too many gifted children who develop in a lopsided manner and come to grief in their lonely worlds. Such superior intelligence creates serious problems of personal and social adjustments. It is necessary to meet *all* the child's basic needs and to provide appropriate, balanced outlets for the superior intelligence. There are classes for gifted children, but Dibs' behavior was not yet mature enough to make him eligible—or, indeed, for such an experience to be particularly good for him.

Dibs was deeply involved in his search for a self. One thing at a time and confidence in the inner resources of this child were imperative. The atmosphere around him should be relaxed, optimistic, sensitive.

"We had a little program at school the other day," Hedda said, with a smile. "It was in the assembly room for the other children in the lower school. We weren't sure whether or not Dibs was ready for this kind of an experience and we decided to leave it entirely up to him. In fact, we decided to have every child in the group make up his mind if he wanted to be in the program or not. It was a story the group had made up and acted out, making up the words and music as they went along. And it was never the same way twice. Every day we would plan it differently. Who wants to be the tree? Who wants to be the wind? Who wants to be the sun? You know how such plays are made up. And then we would let the group decide who should have what part on the day we gave the program in the auditorium.

"We didn't know how Dibs would feel about this or what he would do. We do a lot of this sort of thing and in the past Dibs always ignored us. But he joined the circle and volunteered to do a dance one day. He made one up, much to the delight of the other children. He wanted to be the wind. He went blowing and swaying around and the children all decided that he should be the wind in the school program. Dibs agreed. He did his part very well. Suddenly in the middle of the dance he decided to sing. He made up the words and the melody. It went something like this. 'I am the wind. I blow. I blow. I climb. I climb. I climb the hills and I move the clouds. I bend the trees and I move the grass. No one can stop the wind. I am the wind, a friendly wind, a wind you cannot see. But I am the wind.' He seemed to be unaware of his audience. The children were surprised and delighted. Needless to say, so were we. We thought then that Dibs had at last found himself and was now one of the group."

Dibs was certainly on his way, but I wouldn't say that he had found himself yet. He still had a way to go. His search for self was a tedious, troubled experience that brought him increasing awareness of his feelings and attitudes and relationships with those around him. There were no doubt many feelings that Dibs had not dug out of his past and flung out in his play to know and understand and control better. I hoped that he would find experiences in the playroom that would help him know and feel the

emotions within him in such a way that any hatred and
fear he might have within him would be brought out in
the open and diminished.

Chapter Nineteen

WHEN DIBS CAME FOR his next appointment he asked if he could spend the time in my office. "I noticed that you had a tape recorder," he said. "Will it be all right if I record on it?"

It was quite all right with me, so we went into my office. I put a tape on the recorder, plugged it in, showed Dibs how to operate the recorder. He took the microphone eagerly and turned on the recorder.

"This is Dibs talking," he said. "Listen to me, recorder. You will catch and hold my voice. I am Dibs talking. I am Dibs. This is me." He clicked it off, rewound it, and listened to the recording. He snapped it off and grinned at me. "That was my voice," he said. "I talked and it recorded me. I'll make a long recording and we'll keep it forever and ever. This will be just for us."

He started the recorder again and began to speak into the microphone. He gave his full name, address, telephone number. Then he gave the full name of every member of his family including his grandmother. "I am Dibs and I want to talk," he added. "I am in an office with Miss A and there is a tape recorder here and I am talking into it now. I go to school." He named the school and gave the address. "There are teachers in my school." Each teacher's name was recorded in full. "There are children in my room and I will tell you the names of all the children." He called out the names of all the children. "Marshmallow is our rabbit and a nice rabbit, but he is kept in a cage. Too bad for poor Marshmallow. When I am in school I read and write and count. Now, how is it that I count? One,

two, three, four." The numbers came out slowly and
haltingly. "What comes after four? Yes, I'll help you,
Dibs. Five comes after four. It's one, two, three, four,
five. My! How good you are to be able to count like
that!" Dibs clapped his hands.

"I hear somebody coming in the door," he continued.
"That is too much noise. Be quiet when you are in the
house. Oh, it is Papa. What do you mean by slamming
that door, Papa? You are stupid and careless. I don't want
you around me when you act like that. I don't care what
you want. I'll make you go in your room and I'll lock you
up so we don't have to listen to a screaming, stupid
man!"

Dibs clicked off the recorder and went over to the
window. "It is a nice day outside," he said. "Miss A, why
is it always a nice day when I am here?"

"Does it always seem like a nice day when you come
here?" I asked.

"Yes," he answered. "Even when it is cold or rains, it is
always a nice day in here. Let me play the recording for
you."

He rewound the tape and played it back from the
beginning, listening to it with a serious expression on his
face. He replayed the father's screams several times, then
played it to the end. He clicked it off. "Papa doesn't like
to be sent to his room," he told me. "He doesn't like to be
called stupid." He went to the window again.

"From this window I can see some trees," he said. "I
can count eight trees or some part of them. It's a good
thing to have trees around. They are so tall and
friendly."

He went back to the recorder and turned it on again.
"Once upon a time there was a boy who lived in a big
house with his mother and father and sister. And one day
the father came home and went to his study and the boy
went in without knocking. 'You are a mean man,' the boy
cried. 'I hate you! I hate you! Do you hear me? I hate
you!' And the father began to cry. 'Please,' he said. 'I'm
sorry. I'm sorry for everything I ever did. Please don't

hate me!' But the little boy said to him, 'I am going to punish you, you stupid, stupid man. I don't want you around any more. I want to get rid of you." He clicked off the recorder and came over to me.

"This is only make-believe," he said. "I'm just making up a story about Papa. I made a blotter for him at school. And I tied it with a red ribbon. Then I made an ashtray out of clay and baked it and painted it and I gave it to Papa."

"You made some gifts for Papa? And this story is just make-believe?" I remarked.

"Yes. But let's listen to it."

He played back his story. Then he added to his recording, "This is Dibs talking. I hate my father. He is mean to me. He doesn't like me. He doesn't want me around. I'll tell you who he is and you look out for him. He is a mean, very, very mean man." He again gave his father's full name and address. "He is a scientist," he continued. "He is a very busy man. He wants everything quiet. He does not like the boy. The boy does not like him." He clicked off the recording and came over to me.

"He isn't mean to me any more," he said. "But he used to be mean to me. Maybe he even likes me now." Back to his recording he went. "I hate you, Papa!" he shouted. "I hate you! Don't you ever lock me up again or I'll kill you. I'll kill you anyhow! For all the mean things you did to me!"

He rewound the tape, took it off, and handed it to me. "Put this away," he said. "Put it in the box and put it away and keep it just for us."

"All right. I'll put it away and keep it just for us," I told him.

"I want to go to the playroom," he said. "We'll get this over once and for all."

We went down to the playroom and Dibs jumped into the sandbox and began to dig a deep hole in the sand. Then he went over to the doll house and got the father doll. "Do you have anything to say?" he demanded of the doll. "Are you sorry for all the mean angry things you said?" He shook the doll, threw it around in the sandbox, hit it with the shovel. "I'm going to make a prison for you with a big lock on the door," he said. "You'll be sorry for all the mean things you did."

He got the blocks and began to line the hole with the blocks, building the prison for the father doll. He worked quickly and efficiently. "Please don't do this to me," he cried out for the father doll. "I'm sorry I ever hurt you. Please give me another chance."

"I will punish you for everything you have ever done!" Dibs cried out. He put the father doll down in the sand and came over to me.

"I used to be afraid of Papa," he said. "He used to be very mean to me."

"You used to be afraid of him?" I said.

"He isn't mean to me any more," Dibs said. "But I am going to punish him anyhow!"

"Even though he isn't mean to you now, you still want to punish him?" I said.

"Yes," Dibs answered. "I'll punish him."

Back to the sandbox he went and proceeded to build his prison. Then he placed the father doll in the prison, put a small board over the top, and covered it with the sand. "Who will take care of you?" he cried. Dibs looked at me. "That is the father," he said. "He says he is sorry. Who will buy you things and take care of you? I am your father! Please don't hurt me. I am sorry for all I ever did to you! Oh, I am so sorry. Please, Dibs, please forgive me! I am so sorry." He continued to shovel on the sand and the father doll was buried in his prison.

Dibs walked over to me and drew my arm around his waist. "He is my father," he said. "He takes care of me. But I am punishing him for all the things he did to me that made me sad and unhappy."

"You're punishing him for all the things he used to do that made you so unhappy?" I said.

Dibs walked back to the doll house and picked up the boy doll. "The boy hears his father calling for help and he runs to help him out," he said. Dibs jumped back into the sandbox with the boy doll. "You see. This is Dibs," he said, holding up the boy doll for me to see. "And he goes into this big wilderness and looks for the mountain that has buried his father in that prison and the little boy starts to dig. He digs and digs." Dibs picked up the shovel and dug down to the prison. He lifted the board and peeked into the hole. "Yep. There he is!" Dibs announced. "And he is so sorry for everything he ever did. He says 'I love you, Dibs. Please help me. I need you.' So the little boy un-locks the prison and lets his father out." Dibs carefully picked out the father doll. He held the father doll and the boy doll in his hands and studied them quietly. He took them back to the doll house and placed them side by side on a bench.

Dibs wiped the sand from his hands and once again retreated to the window where he looked out in silence.

"The boy rescued his father and the father was sorry for everything he did that had hurt the boy," I said. "He said he loved Dibs and needed him."

Dibs turned toward me, a little smile playing around the corners of his mouth. "I talked to Papa today," he said, quietly.

"You did? What did you talk about?" I asked.

"Well, he was in the breakfast room finishing up his coffee and reading the morning paper. I walked right up to him and I said, 'Good morning, Papa. You have a nice time today.' And he put down his paper and he said to me, 'Good morning, Dibs. You have a nice time, too.'

And I did. I had a real good time today."

He walked around the playroom, smiling happily.

"Papa took us out to the beach on Sunday in the car. We went way out on Long Island and I saw the ocean. Papa and I walked out to the edge of the water and he told me all about the ocean and the tides and the differences between oceans, lakes, rivers, brooks, and ponds. Then I started to build a sand castle and he asked if he could help me and I gave him my shovel and we took turns. I went in wading, but it was cold and I didn't stay in long. We had a picnic lunch in the car. We had a happy time and Mother just smiled and smiled."

"You had a good time out with your father and moth-er," I commented.

"Yes," Dibs said. "It was nice. A very nice trip out to the beach and back. And there were no angry words. Not any."

"And no angry words," I commented.

He walked over to the sandbox and sat down on the edge of it. "This is where I made a prison for him and where I locked him in and buried him over with sand. I asked myself why I should let him out of his prison and set him free. And then I told myself to just let him be. Just let him be free?"

"Then you decided he should be set free?"

"Yes. I didn't want to keep him locked up and buried. I just wanted to teach him a lesson."

"I understand. You just wanted to teach him a lesson," I commented.

Dibs smiled. "Today I talked to Papa," he said with a happy, relieved smile.

It is interesting to note that Dibs' expressions of venge-ance and hate were expressed more openly and directly and fully only after he felt more secure in his relationship with his father. It was good to hear that he was having more satisfying experiences with his father, who not only poured out information about oceans and rivers and streams but took turns with the shovel and helped build the sand castle with his son.

Chapter Twenty

"HERE I AM AGAIN!" Dibs exclaimed when he came into the waiting room the following Thursday. "There won't be many more times to come before we go away for the summer."

"Yes. About three more times, counting today," I said. "Then we will both go away for a vacation."

"We go way out on the island," Dibs said. "I expect to like my vacation this year. And Grandmother plans to spend the summer with us this year instead of her usual vacation time. I like that idea."

He walked around the playroom. Then he picked up the doll. "Well, here is sister," he exclaimed, as though he had never seen the doll before. "Isn't she a brat of a thing? I'm going to get rid of her. I'll get her to eat some nice rice pudding only I will have poison in it and I'll poison her and she'll go away to stay forever and ever."

"You want to get rid of the sister?" I remarked.

"Sometimes she screams and scratches and hurts me and I'm afraid of her. Sometimes I hit and scratch her. But she isn't home very much. Pretty soon though, she'll be home and she'll be with us for the summer. She's five now."

"Sometimes you both hit and scratch each other, hum?"

"Yes," Dibs said. "But she isn't home very much. She was home this past weekend."

"And how did things go then?" I asked.

"Oh," Dibs shrugged. "I don't mind. Sometimes I played with her. But I won't let her come into my room. I have too many treasures in there. And she tries to snatch and grab and tear them up. Then we fight. But not much any more. She is going to come home to live next year. She'll go to the same school I go to next year."

"And how do you feel about that?" I asked.

"Well, I don't care," Dibs said. "I think I'm glad she's coming home to stay. She must have been very lonesome away at school. "It's my great-aunt's school where she's been. But everybody thinks she should come home."

"And you are glad she is coming home to live?"

"Yes. I really am," Dibs replied. "She doesn't bother me like she used to. When I am playing with my blocks and trains and cars and erector set, she sometimes comes over and plays with me. She hands me a block or a piece of the erector set. She doesn't try to knock down everything I build any more. Then sometimes I play with her. Sunday I read her a story. It was a new book Papa brought home for me. It is the story of electricity. She said she didn't think it was very interesting, but I thought it was. I told her she should pay attention and learn everything she could. I thought it was an exciting story. Papa said he was in a bookstore and he saw this new book for children and he thought I would like it. I did like it."

He went over to the table and started to pound on some clay. "Pretty soon it will be summertime," he said. "I'll go out to the beach and have fun. But first I have something to do."

He went over to the easel and picked up a jar of paint and a glass. He poured some paint into the glass, added a little water, stirred it slowly and carefully. Then he added other colors to the mixture, stirring it well. "This is poison for the sister," he said. "She'll think it is cereal and she'll eat it and then that will be the end of her."

"So that is poison for the sister and after she eats it, then that will be the end of her?"

Dibs nodded. Then he looked at me. "I won't give it to her just yet a while," he said. "I'll wait and think it over."

He walked over to the doll house and took out the mother doll. "What have you done to the boy?" he de-

manded of this doll. "What have you done to him? You
are stupid and I have told you the same thing over and
over and over again. Aren't you ashamed of yourself?" He
carried the mother doll over to the sandbox. "You build
me a mountain!" he demanded. "You stay right there and
you build it and you do it right. The boy will stand guard
to see that you do it right. You better be careful because I
am watching you every minute. Oh God! Oh God! Why is
he like this? What have I done to deserve it? You build
that mountain and don't you tell me you can't do it. I'll
show you how. I'll show you again and again and again.
And you must do it!"

He dropped the mother doll down in the sand and went
over to the window. "It's too hard to do," he said. "Nobody can build a mountain. But I'll make her do it. She'll
have to build the mountain and do it right. There is a
right way and a wrong way to do things. And you will do
it the right way!"

He wandered over to the table and picked up the
nursing bottle. He sucked on it for a long time, while he
looked at me solemnly. "I'm just a baby," he said. "I can't
do anything at all. Somebody has to take care of me and
I'll be baby. Baby don't have to be afraid. Grandmother
take care of baby." He took the nursing bottle out of his
mouth and placed it on the table in front of him.

"Mother can't build the mountain," he said quietly.
"And babies can't build mountains. Nobody can build a
mountain."

"Mother can't? And babies can't? Does it seem to be
just too much to do?" I asked.

"A big storm could come and blow everybody away,"
he said.

"It could?"

"Only I don't want it to," Dibs said softly. "I don't
want anybody blown away."

"I understand."

"Why don't you build that mountain?" Dibs shouted
again. "Why don't you do what you are told? If you
scream and cry, I'll lock you in your room." He looked at

me. "She tries and tries and tries. She is afraid, because
she does not like to be locked away in her room. She
calls for me to help her." He was standing over the
sandbox, looking down at the mother doll.

"She is trying to build the mountain and she is afraid
because she doesn't like to be locked in her room? She is
asking you to help her?" I commented.

"Yes," Dibs said quietly. He went over to the doll he
had identified as the sister. He cuddled her in his arms.
"Have you been afraid, poor little sister?" he said gently.
"I'll take care of you. I'll give you the baby bottle and it
will comfort you." He held the bottle to the doll's lips and
rocked the doll gently in his arms. "Poor little sister. I'll
take care of you. I'll let you come to my party. Nobody
will ever hurt you."

He carried the doll over to the doll bed, gently laid it
down and covered it carefully, but he brought the nursing
bottle back to the table and sucked on the nipple.

"You will help the sister," I commented.

"Yes," he answered. "I'll take care of her." He was
silent for a long time.

"Two of our fish at school died today," he said. "We
don't know what happened to them. Hedda said they were
dead this morning."

"Is that so?" I remarked.

"I made a book for mother in school today," he said.
"She likes flowers and so I cut out pictures of flowers from
a seed catalog. I pasted them on colored paper and printed
the name of the flower under each picture. Then I sewed
all the pages together with green yarn."

"That's interesting. Then what did you do with it?"

"It's still at school," Dibs said. "I'm going to make
something for Papa. And I'm trying to think of something
for Dorothy. When I have something for each one, I'll
take them all home."

"So you plan to make a gift for each one of them?"

"That's my plan," Dibs said. "Only I can't decide what
to make for my sister. I'm making Papa a paper-
weight."

"You want to make something for each member of your family?"

"Yes. I don't want anyone left out," he said. "I'm giving Grandmother a little piece of the tip-end branch of my favorite old tree."

"Grandmother should be pleased with that."

"She will be. It is one of my treasures," Dibs said.

He walked back to the sandbox. "Why Mother!" he cried. "What are you doing down there all alone? You don't have to build a mountain. Come here. I'll help you." He gently cradled the mother doll in his hands. He came up to me. "Sometimes she used to cry," he said in a very low voice. "There would be tears in her eyes and they would run down her face and she would cry. I think maybe she was sad."

"Perhaps she was sad," I said.

"I'll put her back in the house with the family," he announced. "I'll put them all around the dining-room table where they can be together."

I watched him as he carefully placed the family of dolls around the table in the doll house. He knelt down beside the doll house and sang softly to them.

"We gather together to ask the Lord's blessing." The words stopped abruptly. "No. I can't sing that song," he said. "That is only for Grandmother. These are not church people."

He crossed over to the easel and painted splashes of bright color on the paper. "This means happiness," he said. His brush swept the colors across his painting. "The colors are all happy and they are all together, nice and friendly. There will be only two more Thursdays after this," he said.

"Yes. Two more and then the summer vacation. Perhaps you could come back for another visit in the fall if you wanted to," I said.

"I'll miss you," he said. "I'll miss coming. Will you miss me?"

"Yes, I'll miss you, Dibs."

He patted my hand and smiled. "We'll both be away for the summer," he said.

"Yes, we will."

"It's a wonderful playroom," he said. "It's a happy room."

It had been at times a happy room for Dibs, but there had been some sorrowful moments for him, too, as he dug around among his feelings, reliving past experiences that had hurt him deeply.

As Dibs stood before me now his head was up. He had a feeling of security deep inside himself. He was building a sense of responsibility for his feelings. His feelings of hate and revenge had been tempered with mercy. Dibs was building a concept of self as he groped through the tangled brambles of his mixed-up feelings. He could hate and he could love. He could condemn and he could pardon. He was learning through experience that feelings can twist and turn and lose their sharp edges. He was learning responsible control as well as expression of his feelings. Through this increasing self-knowledge, he would be free to use his capacities and emotions more constructively.

Chapter Twenty-One

I HAD BORROWED A WORLD test set and it was in the playroom when Dibs came in the following week. This material consists of many detailed miniature figures of people, animals, buildings, trees, hedges, cars, airplanes, and the like. It was designed primarily as a personality test, but I was not going to use it for this purpose with Dibs. I thought he would be interested in the tiny figures and if he chose to use it, his play would be interesting. I did not intend to suggest that he use it—or, indeed, do anything to direct his activities with any specific material. It was there to be used if he chose to do so.

He immediately noticed the suitcase containing the material and opened it quickly. "We've something new in here," he cried. "Oh look at all these little things." He sorted through the materials quickly. "There are little people and buildings and animals. What is it?"

"You can build a world with it, if you want to," I said. "There's a sheet to spread out on the floor and those blue strips are for water."

"Oh, I say! This is very interesting!" he exclaimed. "This can be a toy town. I can build it anyway I want to build it."

"Yes. You can."

Dibs spread out the sheet, then sat down on the floor beside the materials. He sorted through the figures carefully. He selected a church, a house, and a truck. "I'll build my world," he said happily. "I like these little buildings and people and things. I'll tell you the story I'm building while you watch it grow."

He picked up the tiny white church. "This is the church, a big, white church. A church for God and the little people. And these are city things." He picked out houses, trucks, cars. "These city things—the houses and the trucks are filled with a rush of noise. It is the noise of the city." He began to lay out the streets. "The houses are going up one after another. This is a whole city. And this is a little, quiet back street. Now here is a road going out to the airport and the airport is close to the water. I'll put airplanes here in the airport. Out here on the water, I'll put these little boats. Oh! Look! These are street signs. This is Second Avenue and there is a Second Avenue here in New York. And this is a stop-and-go sign." Dibs was absorbed in building his world. "Here is go and here is stop. And this is a fence and this is a hedge. And this airplane is flying all around." He zoomed the airplane around with a flourish.

"The boat is here on the river. It swims up and down on the river. Now there are three airplanes at the airport. And here is a hotel. Now where will I put the hotel? I will put it here and out in front of it I'll put the newsman's wagon. Then I'll put some more houses over here. Now for some stores. Because people have to have stores. Where are they? Here they are. And here is a hospital and a garage. There's everything in here that I need to make my world," Dibs said.

"It looks that way," I remarked.

"This hospital is a big building. I'll put it here on First Avenue. That's what this street sign says. Yes. That will be the hospital. For sick people. And it smells like sickness and medicine and it is a sad place to be. Now here is a nice house and it is on the south side of the street. This is a whole big, loud city and it needs a park. Right here I'll make a park. I'll put out these trees and bushes. Here is the school. No." He put the school back in the box. "This is another house. All these houses are close together and people live in them. They are neighbors and they are friendly. Now I'll put a fence around the airport. I'll fence that in for safety. And now the hedges." He picked out the green sponge-rubber hedges. "These are all growing plants. Hedges and trees. Lots of trees. All in a row down the avenue. All these trees with leaves on them. A city in the summertime."

He sat back on his heels and looked at me. He stretched out his arms and smiled. "The lovely, leafy summertime! Now out on the edge of the city is a farm. I'll put some cows out there." He lined up the cows. "They are all going to the barn. They are all lined up waiting to be milked." He bent over the box and sorted out more figures.

"Now for the people!" he cried. "A city has to have people. And here is the mailman." He held the figure out for me to see. "He has a bag full of letters and you see he moves around and stops at every house. Everyone gets a letter all his own. And Dibs—even Dibs gets a letter all his own. Then he goes over here to the hospital so the sick and hurt people get mail, too. And when they do they smile inside. The truck drives up to the airport. This fence keeps the airplanes in so they won't roll out and hurt people. And this airplane is flying off up in the sky." He flew a plane over his city. "Look!" he cried. "Over the city, over the city it goes. The big airplane cutting Pepsi Cola holes in the blue sky so the white heaven shines through. Then the farmer goes out to see. . . ." Dibs broke off his play and sat there quietly looking at the world he was building. He sighed. He took other figures out of the suitcase.

"Here are the children and their mother," he said. "They live together on a farm in a friendly house. Here are some little lambs and chickens. And here is mother going down the road, down the street to the city. I wonder where she is going? Maybe she is going to the butcher shop to get some meat. No. She is going down the street and on and on until she is right beside the hospital. Now I wonder why she is standing there by the hospital?"

"I wonder, too," I said.

Dibs sat very still for a long time, looking at the mother figure. "Well," he said at last. "There she is and she is right beside the hospital. There are a lot of cars running down the streets and a fire engine. Everything has to get out of the way of the fire engine." He shoved the cars and the fire engine up and down the streets, making noises for them.

"Now then. Where are the children? Oh, here is one child. He is going down to the river alone. Poor little child so all alone. And the alligator swims in that river. And here is a big snake. Sometimes snakes live in the water. The boy goes down closer and closer to the river. Closer to the danger."

Once again Dibs stopped his activity and looked over his world. Suddenly he smiled. "I am a builder of cities," he said. "This is the cook out emptying the garbage. And this woman is going to the store. But this woman is going to church to sing a song for she is a good woman." He placed another child beside the one already standing on the river shore. "This child is going after the boy," he explained. "The boy is wading in the river now and he doesn't know about the alligator and the snake. But the other boy was a friend and he called a warning to him and told him to get in a boat. The boy did get into the boat. See? And the boat is safe. The two boys get in the boat together and they are friends." He placed the two boys in a boat.

"Now here is a policeman stopping and going the traffic. This is for everybody's good." He placed more street signs around in his city. "Some of the streets go up and down, but some of the streets go only one way and this street is a one-way street." Dibs took the school out of the box. "This says School Number One. We have to have a school. The children must have a school to go to." He laughed. "A school so they can be educated. This child here—this little girl—she will stay at home. She will stay at home with her mother and her father and her brother. They want her home so she will not be lonesome." He selected all the tiny figures of people and placed them around in the world he was building. He had created a world filled with people.

"Here is home," he said, indicating one of the houses. "There is a big tree in the back yard. It is a very special tree. And this man is coming down the street. He is coming home. He is the father."

Dibs got up and went across the room to the pegboard set and pounded the pegs with vigor. "I have new toys to play with," he said. "I have a city to build with houses and people and animals. I built a city—a big, crowded city all squeezed together like New York. Someone is certainly doing a lot of typing out in that office."

He went back to his city and dropped down on the floor beside it. "The dump truck is coming down this street and the traffic sign says stop but when the policeman sees the truck he turns the sign to say go and the truck goes happily on its way. A dog comes down the street and the policeman turns the sign so the dog doesn't have to wait and so the dog goes happily on. Stop. Go. Stop. Go. I tell you there is life in this city. Things move. People come and go. Houses and churches and cars and people and animals and stores. Then way out here animals on a cool, green farm."

Suddenly he picked up the fire engine and zoomed it down the street. "The fire truck is called because the house is on fire and the people are caught upstairs—the grown people. They scream and yell and they can't get out. But the fire truck comes and pours on water. They are as scared as they can be but they are safe."

Dibs laughed softly to himself. "Why that was your father, Dibs. And that was your mother."

He came over to the table and sat down, looking at me. "Father is still so very, very busy," he said. "Doctor Bill came to see mother the other day. They used to be very good friends. He stayed a long time and talked to Mommy. Doctor Bill likes my Mommy. Doctor Bill said I was all right."

"He did?"

"Yep. Out of the woods, he said. Whatever that means. When I leave here today I have to go to the barber shop and get my hair cut. I used to yell and carry on, but I don't any more. Once I bit the barber."

"You did?"

"Yep. I was afraid, but I'm not afraid any more."

"So you are not afraid any more?" I remarked.

"I guess maybe I am growing up," Dibs said. "But I must finish my town. I'm going to put all the trees and bushes and shrubs around so I can make the city beautiful. This is a very busy street. I'm going to put all the people all over the city. Here is a taxi that is meeting the train. People come visiting and everyone is happy to see them. Now here is the mailman. You see he has been up and down every street and brought mail—letters—to all the people. But here is Papa trying to get home and he has to stop for this traffic sign and it says stop. Papa stops and he cannot move until the sign says go, but the sign always says stop and Papa cannot move. There are many trees around. Cities need trees because they give such a friendly shade. Look at my city. My world! I built my world and it is a world full of friendly people."

When it was time to go, Dibs looked back at the world he had built—a world full of friendly people. But "Papa" was stopped dead in his tracks by a traffic sign that would not let him get home. And as he left the playroom there was a little smile on his lips as he left "Papa" immobilized in his world of friendly people.

Dibs had built a well-organized world, full of people and action. His plan showed high intelligence, a grasp of the whole as well as the details of his concepts. There was purpose, integration, creativity in his design. The attractive miniature figures intrigued him. He had built a highly developed, meaningful world. There had been hostile feelings expressed directly at the mother and father concepts. There had been expressions of responsible awareness. Dibs was growing up.

Chapter Twenty-Two

WHEN DIBS CAME IN for his last session before summer vacation he asked if he could spend part of his time in my office. He sat down at my desk and gazed at me seriously. "This is my last Thursday," he said.

"Yes. It is."

"I'll go away for the summer. We'll be at the beach. There will be lots of trees out in the country—but no trees at the beach. The water is so blue. I like it out there. But I'll miss coming here. I'll miss you," he said.

"I'll miss you, Dibs. It's been very nice to know you."

"I want to see if my name is on a card in your file."

"Look and see."

He did. His name was there. "Will you always keep it?" he asked. "Will you always remember me?"

"Yes, Dibs. I'll always remember you."

"Do you have the tape that I recorded?"

"Yes. I have the tape."

"Let me see it once more."

I got the tape out of the filing cabinet and handed him the box. His name was written on it.

"You have been recorded, Dibs," he said. "You made this tape talk. This tape catching and holding my voice. This is my voice on tape."

"Yes. That's the recording you made."

"May I put some more words on the tape?" he asked.

"If you want to."

"I want to. I'll catch and hold my voice on that tape. I like the recorder."

We put the tape on the recorder and listened to the part

he had previously recorded. Then he clicked it on for additional recording.

"This is my last visit to the playroom," he said, speaking into the microphone. "This is Dibs talking. This is my voice. I came to the playroom. I did so many things in the playroom. I am Dibs." There was a long pause. "I am Dibs," he repeated slowly. "Maybe in the fall I will come back again for a visit. Maybe for just one more visit after the summer. I am going away for the summer and I will be beside the ocean. I will listen to the waves. I will play in the sand."

There was another long pause. Then he clicked off the recorder. "Let's go back to the playroom," he said. "I want to play with the world set again."

We went back to the playroom. Dibs got out the materials and began once again to build his town. Quickly he laid out the buildings and trees. He placed the other figures around through the town. Then he selected four buildings and placed them carefully. "See these two houses?" he said. "This is a house. And this is a house. This building is a jail and this is a hospital." He placed the two houses side by side. "This is your house and this is my house," he said, indicating the two houses. "Mine is all white and green. There are trees and flowers and singing birds all around it. All the doors and all the windows are wide open. You live right next door to me. You have a very fine house, too. And all around your house are flowers and trees and singing birds. There is no fence and no hedge between your house and my house."

He sorted through the buildings and picked out the tiny church. He placed it in back of his house. "Here is the church," he said. "It is back of my house." He moved it a little so that it was placed midway between the two houses. "It is between and in back of both our houses," he said. "We share the church. We share the chimes. And we both listen to the church music. Now here is the jail. It is across from my house. And here is the school. You see, we share the church and we share the school, but the jail

is all mine. You have nothing to do with jails. You do not
like jails. You have no use for jails. But I do. And there is
a big horse chestnut tree in my back yard. This is the
summertime and there are so many trees—cool, green,
leafed-out trees for the wind to blow through." He spread
out his arms like branches and swayed gently in the wind
he imagined.

Suddenly he got up and paced the room. He looked out
the window. "There are cars parked out there," he said. "I
cannot see any other person now out this window."

He seemed a little upset, but he returned to his city,
dropped down on the floor and started to move some of
the figures. "Here is Jail Street," he said. "There are no
trees around the jail. It is down here, away from other
friendly houses and away from the church. It is lonely and
cold. But this church is close to our houses," he announced, touching the church steeple. "There is a cross on
the top of the church to tell directions. But this building
here is the jail. And Papa is going to this jail. My Papa.
His office is on the first floor of the jail." Dibs laughed. He
buzzed some little cars up and down the streets. He
hummed a little song. He picked up the mother, father,
girl, and boy figures and held them in his hands. "These
are the people," he said. "This is the father, the mother,
the sister, the boy. Now the father is standing by your
house. He doesn't know what to do. And this is the
mother. And this boy is Dibs. This little girl is with her
father. She is going to jail. The sister and mother are going
to jail—because I don't need a sister." He threw the girl
doll back in the box.

He got up and paced the room, sighing deeply. "Sunday
I usually stay home all day," he said. "Sunday is a nothing
day. Jake said Sunday was a sacred day. But see this jail?"
He picked it up and held it out to me.

"Yes. I see the jail."

"It is a one-way jail," Dibs said. "It's a one-way jail on
a one-way street. And there is no going back after you get
put in jail. Sister is gone now."

"Yes. I notice. Sister is gone now."

"It's too crowded in the city," Dibs announced. "Out they go—spreading out toward the country. And all these houses and people begin to move, past Dibs' house, past your house, out to the country."

He placed another house. "This is Grandmother's house," he announced. "There are no trees around her house. She loves trees, so she'll have to walk down here to my house to enjoy the trees."

He sorted through the figures and picked out a man. He studied it carefully. "This is a big boy," he said. "I think he is Dibs. I'll take this little child out and put in the grown-up Dibs." He exchanged the figures. He placed a woman figure on the street. "This is Grandmother," he said. "Good Grandmother. Friendly Grandmother. And the mailman is bringing Dibs a letter. Dibs is grown up now. I think Dibs is as big as Papa." He measured the figures carefully. "Yes. Dibs is as big as father and bigger than mother. There are hedges and plants all around. They grow to beautify the city. Each little green plant helps the city. I'll put fences around the airport for safety. The fire engine is coming down the street, bumping into cars because it is such a busy street. But there are no more fires. Everyone is safe and happy."

He came over to me. "I'll be going away next week," he said. "I'll be gone all summer. Grandmother will spend this summer with us. But when I come back in September I want to come back again for a visit."

"I think we can arrange that," I told him. "And I hope you have a very happy summer."

Dibs grinned. "I got my school yearbook today," he said. "My picture is in it. I'm in the front row between Sammy and Freddy. And there is a story in it that I wrote. I wrote a story about my home and the big friendly tree outside my window. They printed it in the school yearbook. Do you remember what I told you about the big friendly tree?"

"Yes, I remember."

"Birds come there in that tree and I open my window and I talk to them. I send them around the world to different places. I tell them to go to California or London or Rome and sing songs and make people happy. I love the birds. We're friends. But right now I have something else I must do. I must get my sister out of the box and decide what I shall do with her. She has to stay at home. And when the father comes home from his office he scolds her. Then the sister goes to live with the pigs. And so does the mother." He laughed. "Not really," he said. "They live together in a house. The mother, the father, the sister, and the boy." He picked up the little boy he had designated as Dibs and the grown-up Dibs figure. He held them both in his hands. "Here is little Dibs and grown-up Dibs," he said. "This is me and this is me."

"I see. You are little Dibs and grown-up Dibs," I commented.

"And here is a woman walking down the street. She comes to my house. Who is she? Why she is Miss A. She lives here with Dibs. And the sister lives here with her father. She has no mother. Just a father who buys her the things she needs but who leaves her alone while he goes to work. The mother fell in the river. But she got out safely— only very wet and very frightened. This woman here is walking down the street. She is going to church. She is doing right." He placed the figure near the church. "And these men are going to war. They will go fighting. There will be wars and fighting always, I guess. But these four people are a family and they decide to go on an outing together and they do. They take a ride to the beach and they are happy. They are all together and they feel happy. Then Grandmother comes and all five of them are happy together."

Dibs bent over his city and moved the jail. "The jail is right next to Miss A's house now and she says she does not like jails and she takes it far away and buries it in the sand and there isn't a jail any more for any one." Dibs buried the jail in the sandbox. "Then there are these two houses. Your house and my house and they begin to slowly move farther and farther apart." He slowly moved the two houses apart. "My house and Miss A's house are getting farther and father apart—about a mile afar. And the sister is now Miss A's little girl. She comes to her house for visits." He placed the sister and Miss A together beside the house.

"It is very early in the morning and big Dibs is going to school. He has friends in school. But this little boy is little Dibs." He held this figure in his hand and studied it carefully. "This little boy is very sick. He goes to the hospital and he is melting away. He is shrinking littler and littler until he is all gone." He went over and buried the figure in the sand. "The little boy is gone now," he said. "But big Dibs is big and strong and brave. He is not afraid any more." He looked up at me.

"Big and strong and brave and not afraid any more," I said.

He sighed. "We will say goodbye today," he said. "I won't be back for a long time. You'll go away and I'll go away. We'll take vacations. And I am not afraid any more."

Dibs had come to terms with himself. In his symbolic play he had poured out his hurt, bruised feelings, and had emerged with feelings of strength and security. He had gone in search of a self that he could claim with proud identity. Now he was beginning to build a concept of self that was more in harmony with the capacities within him. He was achieving personal integration.

The feelings of hostility and revenge that he expressed toward his father, mother, and sister still flared up briefly, but they did not burn with hatred or fear. He had exchanged the little, immature, frightened Dibs for a self-concept strengthened by feelings of adequacy, security, and courage. He had learned to understand his feelings. He had learned how to cope with them and to control them. Dibs was no longer submerged under his feelings of fear and anger and hatred and guilt. He had become a person in his own right. He had found a sense of dignity and self-respect. With this confidence and security, he could learn to accept and respect other people in his world. He was no longer afraid to be himself.

Chapter Twenty-Three

I DID NOT GET back from my vacation until the first of October. There were messages waiting for me. One was from Dibs' mother. I called her, anxious to learn what experiences the summer had brought to this family.

"Dibs wants one more visit," she said. "The first of September he told me he wanted another visit with you, but I explained that you would not be back until October. He didn't mention it again until the first of this month. Then he said 'Mother, it is now October first. You said Miss A would be back then. Call her up and tell her I want one more visit and then no more.' So, I'm calling." She laughed softly.

"He has been wonderful," she said. "We've had a wonderful summer. I can never tell you how happy and grateful we are. He isn't like the same child. He's happy, relaxed. He relates to all of us very well. He talks all the time. He doesn't really need to come in again and if you are too busy just say so and I'll explain it to Dibs."

Needless to say, I was not too busy to see Dibs again. I set up the appointment for the following Thursday.

Dibs came in with a happy step, a bright smile, shining eyes. He stopped and talked to the secretaries in the outer office who were typing and transcribing recordings. He asked them what they were doing and if they liked their work. "Are you happy?" he asked them. "You should be happy!"

There was a marked change in him since his last visit. He was relaxed, out-going, happy. There was grace and spontaneity in his movements. When I came out to the waiting room to meet him he rushed over to me and held out his hand to shake hands.

"I wanted to see you once more," he said. "And here I am. Let's go first into your office."

We did. He stood in the middle of the room and looked around. There was a big smile on his face. He ran around and touched the desk, the filing cabinets, the chairs, the bookshelves. He sighed. "Oh what a wonderful, happy place," he said.

"You have enjoyed being here, haven't you," I remarked.

"Oh yes," Dibs said. "So very, very much. There are so many wonderful things in here."

"What wonderful things?" I asked.

"Books!" Dibs said. "Books and books and books." He lightly ran his fingers over the books. "I love books," he said. "And isn't it funny that little black marks on paper can be so good? Pieces of paper and little tiny black marks and you've got a story."

"Yes," I replied. "It is quite remarkable."

"That's right," Dibs said.

He looked out the window. "It is a pretty day. And this is such a nice window for looking out of."

He sat down at the desk, reached over for the card file, examined the cards, and smiled broadly. "Why you have left it just you and Dibs," he exclaimed. "There is nobody else in this box but you and me. Just the two of us."

"Isn't that what you said you wanted?" I asked.

"Yes. Just that way. Did you throw out everybody else's card?" he asked.

"No. I put them in another box. In that card file over there."

"But this one you kept just for us?"

"As you said you wanted it," I replied.

Dibs leaned back in the desk chair and looked at me for a long time. There was a sober expression on his face. "That's the way it's always been," he said, slowly. "As you said you wanted it," he repeated. Then he smiled. "As I said I wanted it," he exclaimed.

He reached over and selected a clean card. He picked up a pencil and wrote something on the card. Bent over it, he carefully and deliberately printed something on the card. Then he handed it to me. "Read it," he said. "Read it to me."

"Goodbye dear room with all the nice books. Goodbye dear desk. Goodbye window with sky showing through. Goodbye cards. Goodbye dear lady of the wonderful playroom," I read his message to him.

He reached for the card. "I want to add something," he said. He printed something on the back of the card and handed it to me. Three lines he had written: "As you said you wanted it. As I said I wanted it. As we said we wanted it."

After I read it, he took it and filed it away with our two cards.

"Let's go back to the playroom," he said. "Let us go! Let us go! Oh, let us go!"

He entered the playroom with a rush, flung his arms wide, whirled around, laughed. "Oh what fun! What fun! What fun!" he cried. "What a wonderful playroom this is!"

He ran over, turned the water on full force and stood back laughing happily. "Water. Water. Water. Come out and gush. Splash all over. Have fun!" Then he turned off the water, smiled at me, and walked over to the easel.

"Hello, paints," he said. "Are you all mixed up? Yep. I see you are." He picked up the jar of yellow paint and turned to me. "You know what?" he asked.

"What?"

"I would like to deliberately pour it on the floor."

"You would? Just deliberately pour it on the floor?"

"Yes," Dibs said. "And what is more I will."

"You not only feel like doing it, but you will do it?"

Dibs unscrewed the lid. He tilted the jar and the paint slowly spilled out on the floor. "It makes a nice puddle of paint," he said.

"You like it, do you?"

"I like pouring it out," he said. "I like getting rid of it."

When the jar was empty, he put it on the sink.

"Now is there any reason why paint should be used just for painting? In a playroom?" he asked me. "I never did like that yellow paint and it makes me feel good to have poured it all out and gotten rid of it. Now I'll get some rags and mop it up." He got out some cleaning rags and wiped up the puddle of yellow paint as best he could.

Then Dibs came over to me. "I can't figure this all out," he said.

"What can't you figure out?" I asked.

"All this. And you. You're not a mother. You're not a teacher. You're not a member of mother's bridge club. What are you?"

"You can't quite figure out just what kind of a person I am, h'm?" I said.

"No, I can't," Dibs said. He shrugged his shoulders. "But it really doesn't matter," he said, slowly gazing straight into my eyes. "You are the lady of the wonderful playroom." He suddenly knelt down and ran his fingers down my leg and looked closely at my mesh hose. "You're the lady with hundreds of tiny holes in your stockings," he said with a shout of laughter.

He jumped up, ran over to the table and picked up the nursing bottle. "Baby bottle," he said. "Dear comforting baby bottle. When I need you, you bring me comfort." He sucked on the nursing bottle for several minutes. "I was a baby again and I loved the nursing bottle. But six-year-old Dibs does not need you now. Goodbye, baby bottle, goodbye."

He looked around the room, found his target in the iron radiator. "Goodbye, baby bottle, goodbye. I do not need you anymore." He hurled the bottle against the radiator and it broke into many pieces. The water in the bottle spilled out on the floor. Dibs went over and looked down at it. "I have finished with it," he said.

"You don't need the baby bottle any more and now you've gotten rid of it?" I remarked.

"Yes. That's right!" Dibs said.

He went over to the sandbox and dug quite vigorously

in the sand. "Bury things. Bury things. Bury things. Then dig them up again, if you feel like it," he laughed. "I tell you this sand is good stuff. It does many things. And you make glass out of sand. I read a book about it."

He walked over to the doll house. He collected the family of dolls and placed them in the living room. "Little old play people. I'll say goodbye to you now. And I'll sit you down here in the living room and you wait until another little child comes here to play with you." He turned and looked at me. "After I go some other child will come here and take my place, won't he?" Dibs asked.

"Another child will come to the playroom," I said.

"You see other children in here besides me, don't you?" he asked.

"Yes. I see other children."

"It will make the children happy," he said.

He went over to the window and opened it. He leaned out and sniffed the air. "Out of this window I saw the world," he said. "I saw the trucks and the trees and the airplanes and the people and the church that chimes one, two, three, four, when it is time to go home."

He walked over to me and spoke almost in a whisper. "Even if I didn't want to go home, it was my home."

He took my hands in his. He looked at me for a long time. "I want to go see that church," he said. "Can we go over there and walk around that church and go inside and look at it?"

"I think we can," I said. It was a most unusual procedure to do so, but it was also a most unusual request. It seemed important on this last visit to grant this request.

We went out of the Center and walked around the outside of the church. Dibs looked up at it, impressed by its tremendous size.

"Now let's go in. Let's see it inside," he said.

We went up the front steps. I opened the huge doors and we went inside. Dibs was dwarfed by the lofty archways. He walked slowly down the center aisle, ran a few steps, stopped, looked up and around him with an expression of complete awe and wonderment on his shining face. He was impressed by the magnificence of the chapel.

"I feel so very, very little," he said. "I think I must have shrunk." He turned slowly and gazed at the beauty around him. "Grandmother says a church is God's house," he said. "Now I have never seen God, but he must be awfully, awfully big to need such a big, big house. And Jake said a church is such a sacred place."

Suddenly he ran down the aisle toward the altar. He threw back his head and stretched both his arms high up toward the big stained glass windows over the chancel. He turned and looked at me, momentarily speechless.

Just at that moment, the organist started to play the pipe organ. Dibs ran to me and grabbed my hand.

"Let us go! Let us go! I am afraid!" he cried.

"Did the music frighten you?" I asked, as we started toward the door.

Dibs stopped and looked back. "Listen. Let's don't go yet," he said.

We stopped.

"I am afraid of the bigness and I am afraid of the noise," Dibs said. "But it is so beautiful it fills me with brightness and beauty."

"Afraid of it, but liking it, too?" I said. "It is a beautiful church."

Dibs let go of my hand and walked down the center aisle again. "What is it that makes that strange noise?" he asked.

"It is a man playing on a pipe organ and that noise is the music of the pipe organ."

"Oh," said Dibs. "I have never heard such music before. It makes me cold. It gives me goose pimples." He held my hand tightly. "I have never seen anything so beautiful," he whispered. The sun was shining through the colored glass and the beams of light stretched out toward us.

"Let's get out of here," Dibs said softly. We walked back to the door. Dibs looked back over his shouldler. At the door he stopped again. "Wait a minute," he whispered. He waved timidly toward the altar and said in a tiny voice, "Goodbye, God. Goodbye!"

We left the church and went back to the playroom. Dibs did not say a word on the way back. When we got into the playroom he sat down in the chair beside the table. He smiled at me. "That was really very nice," he said. "I was in God's house today. For the very first and only time, I was in God's house."

He sat there quietly for a long time, looking down at his folded hands.

"Tell me," he said suddenly. "Why do some people believe in God and some not believe?"

"I don't think I know how to answer that question, Dibs," I said.

"But it is true that some people do believe and some do not?"

"Yes. I think so."

"Grandmother believes. But Papa and Mother are not church-believers. And Jake believed. He told me about it."

"I think everyone makes up his own mind," I said. "Each person decides for himself."

"I wonder what God is like?" Dibs said. "Grandmother told me once God was our Father in heaven. Father is another way of saying Papa. I wouldn't want God to be like Papa. Because sometimes I don't think Papa loves me. And if I believed in God like Grandmother does, I'd want God to love me. But Grandmother says that Papa does love me. But if he does why don't I know it? Grandmother loves me and I love her and I know because I feel it deep inside of me." He clasped his hands together against his heart, gazed into my eyes with a troubled frown wrinkling his forehead. "It's hard to figure things like this out," he concluded, after a long silence. He walked to the window and looked out at the church.

"That is God's house," he said quietly. "Grandmother says God is love. And Jake said he believed in God. He said he prayed which means he talked to God. But I have never prayed. But I would like to talk to God. I would like to hear what He has to say. There's a boy in my room at school who believes in God. He is a Catholic and he believes in God. There's another boy who is a Jew and he goes to a synagogue and that is the house the Jews built for God." He turned and looked at me. He held his arms out toward me, hands outstretched. "But Papa and Mother are not God-believing people and so I am not. It makes me feel lonesome not knowing God." He paced back and forth across the playroom.

"Grandmother is a good woman," he said. "She goes to church and she sings songs about God. She believes." He came over to me and took my hands in his, searching my face eagerly. "Tell me," he said. "Why do some people believe in God and some not believe?"

This was a difficult question to answer. "Everyone makes up his own mind when he is older," I said. "Each person decides for himself what he believes. But right now, it is very confusing to you, isn't it?"

"Yes," he said. "Very confusing." There was a long silence between us.

"Do you know what I am trying to do now?" he asked me.

"No. What?"

"I'm trying to learn how to play baseball. Papa is trying to teach me. We go to the park together. But Papa is no ballplayer, either. The balls are hard things to hit with a bat. And they are hard things to throw where you want them to go. But I'll learn how to do it because all the boys at school play baseball and I want to play with them. So I must know. So I try hard. And I will learn. But I don't like it very well. I can play cops and robbers better and I like running through old Mrs. Henry's yard. She yells at me now, too."

The buzzer rang. Dibs' mother was here to meet him.

"Goodbye, Dibs," I said. "It's been so very nice to know you."

"Yes. It has been," Dibs replied. "Goodbye."

We went to the reception room. He skipped over and

took his mother's hand. "Hello there, Mother," he said. "I'm not coming back anymore. This today was for good-bye."

They left together—a little boy who had the opportunity to state himself through his play and who had emerged a happy, capable child, and a mother who had grown in understanding and appreciation for her very gifted child.

Chapter Twenty-Four

ONE DAY TWO AND a half years later I was sitting in the living room of my apartment reading. It was a ground-floor apartment on the corner of the street. The windows were open and a voice—a very strong, lilting voice—a very familiar child's voice came through the open window.

"I say, Peter May, come down here and look in my yard. There are twenty-seven different shrubs and plants in my yard. Do come and see!"

"Twenty-seven what, huh?"

"Different shrubs and plants in my yard."

"Oh."

"Come and see."

"You look what I got here."

"What is it? Oh. Marbles!"

"Yes. Do you want to trade?"

"Yes. What do you want to trade?"

"What have you got? What have you got, Dibs?"

Yes. It was Dibs and a friend.

"I'll tell you! I'll tell you!" Dibs cried excitedly. "You give me that blue marble there with the snake eye and I'll give you one of the first worms up this spring."

"You will? Where are they?"

"Right here they are!" Dibs dug down into his pocket and brought out a little glass jar, unscrewed the lid with the perforated top, and carefully extracted one worm. He laid it in Peter's grimy hand. He was smiling. Peter was impressed.

"Remember," said Dibs carefully. "This is a real first worm up this spring."

Dibs had apparently moved into the big apartment house with the gardens down the street from me. A few days later I met him on the street. We looked at each other. Dibs smiled a big smile and reached out and touched my hand.

"Hello, you," he said.

"Hello, Dibs."

"I know who you are," he said.

"You do?"

"Oh, yes! You are the lady of the wonderful playroom," he said. "You are Miss A."

We sat down on the front steps of an apartment house along the way to talk.

"Yes," I said. "And you are Dibs."

"I'm grown up now," he said. "But I do remember when I was very, very small and first came to see you. I remember the toys, the doll house and the sand and the men and women and children in the world I built. I remember the bells and the time to go and the truck. I remember the water and the paint and the dishes. I remember our office and our books and our recording machine. I remember all the people. And I remember how you played with me."

"What did we play, Dibs?"

Dibs leaned toward me. His eyes were shining. "Everything I did, you did," he whispered. "Everything I said, you said."

"So that's the way it was!" I said.

"Yes. 'This is your room, Dibs,' you said to me. 'This is all for you. Have fun, Dibs. Have fun. Nobody is going to hurt you. Have fun.'" Dibs sighed. "And I did have fun. I had the most wonderful time in my life. I built my world with you in the playroom. Remember?"

"Yes, Dibs. I remember."

"And the last time I saw you there in the playroom was two years, six months, and four days come Thursday. I remember it very well. I took that last-day sheet out of my calendar and I put a big red circle around it with red crayon. I framed it and it hangs on the wall in my room.

Just the other day I happened to look at it and checked how long ago it was. Two years, six months, four days come Thursday."

"So that day seemed very important to you," I commented. "And you circled it and framed it. Why did you do that, Dibs?"

"I don't know," Dibs said. "I wouldn't ever have forgotten it. I have thought about it many times." There was a long pause. Dibs looked steadily at me. He sighed deeply. "At first the playroom seemed so very, very big. And the toys were not friendly. And I was so afraid."

"You were afraid in there, Dibs?"

"Yes."

"Why were you afraid?"

"I don't know. I was frightened at first because I didn't know what you would do and I didn't know what I would do. But you just said 'This is all yours, Dibs. Have fun. Nobody is going to hurt you in here.' "

"I said that?"

"Yes," Dibs said decisively. "That is what you said to me. And gradually I came to believe you. And it was that way. You said for me to go fight my enemies until they cried out and said they were sorry they hurt me."

"And did you do that?"

"Yes. I found out my enemies and I fought them. But then I found out that I was not afraid anymore. I found out that I am not unhappy when I feel love. Now I am big and strong and not afraid. And I remember the church that last come-back day. I remember discovering how big God was. The door was so very high. And the ceiling was way up there, almost touching heaven. And when the music started to play all of a sudden, I shivered. I wanted to get out and I wanted to stay. And I went past there the other day. I went up all the steps to the door. The door was closed. I knocked on the door and I called through the keyhole. 'Is anyone home today?' But I guess not because nobody came and so I went away."

I could just visualize Dibs walking up the steps of the

church and ·knocking timidly on that massive carved door.

Suddenly he jumped up. "Come see my yard," he cried. "It's a very, very big yard and it's got lots and lots of plants and shrubs in it. Guess how many?"

"Oh," I said. "Twenty-seven different kinds?"

"Yes," Dibs shouted. "But how did you know? I counted them for over two weeks before I knew. Have you ever been in my yard?"

"No. I have not been in your yard," I replied.

"Then how did you know? How *did* you know? You tell me how you knew!"

"You don't think I could know unless I went in and counted them?"

"But," said Dibs, exasperated. "It's even more than counting. You have to look carefully at each plant and shrub and see what way it is different. Then you find out what it is. Then you count them. Write down the name and location of each plant. It is not a quick and simple thing to do. It is not something you can just guess. And if you were never in my yard and never did all this, then how on earth do you know that there are twenty-seven different kinds in there?"

"Well, Dibs, I'll tell you," I said. "The other day I was sitting in my apartment reading by the open window and I heard you tell Peter, 'There are twenty-seven different plants and shrubs in my yard.' It was the day you gave him the first worm up for spring."

"Oh!" Dibs exclaimed. "Because you live nearby. Why Miss A, now we are neighbors!"

"Yes. We are neighbors."

"This is good," Dibs said. "Well, then, so you come now and see my garden." We went into Dibs' yard and he pointed out the twenty-seven different varieties.

A few days later I met his mother and father on the street. We exchanged greetings and his mother and father both thanked me again for the help I had given them. They said that Dibs had continued to make amazing progress, that he was a well-adjusted, happy child, that he was getting along satisfactorily with other children. He was now enrolled in a school for gifted children and was doing very well.

Just at that moment, Dibs came riding around the corner on a bicycle, yelling like an Indian.

"Dibs," His mother called. "Dibs, come see who is here. Do you remember this lady?"

Dibs ran up and grinned. "Hello," he shouted.

"Hello, Dibs," I said.

"Your mother asked you a question, Dibs," said Papa.

"Yes, Papa, I heard her," said Dibs. "She asked me if I knew the lady. Of course, I know the lady. She is my very first friend."

Papa seemed a little embarrassed. "Well, if you heard your mother, why didn't you answer her?"

"I'm sorry, Papa," said Dibs. There was a twinkle in his eye.

"Very nice to have seen you again," "Papa" said to me. "Sorry, but I must go now." He started out toward his car.

Dibs called after him, "You and Mom are a bit full of burrs above your ears because I met Miss A five days ago!"

Papa turned red and disappeared into his car and drove off.

"Mom" looked a little upset. "None of that, Dibs," she said. "And why don't you call her by her full name? Why always Miss A?"

Dibs jumped back on his bicycle.

"Miss A. Miss A. A special name for a special friend," he shouted. He tore down the street, making a noise like a fire engine.

Yes, Dibs had changed. He had learned how to be himself, to believe in himself, to free himself. Now he was relaxed and happy. He was able to be a child.

Epilogue

DIBS HAD HAD HIS dark moments and had lived for a while in the shadows of life. But he had had the opportunity to move out of those dark moments and discover for himself that he could cope with the shadows and sunshine in his life.

Perhaps there is more understanding and beauty in life when the glaring sunlight is softened by the patterns of shadows. Perhaps there is more depth in a relationship that has weathered some storms. Experience that never disappoints or saddens or stirs up feeling is a bland experience with little challenge or variation in color. Perhaps when we experience confidence and faith and hope that we see materialize before our eyes this builds up within us a feeling of inner strength, courage, and security.

We are all personalities that grow and develop as a result of all our experiences, relationships, thoughts, and emotions. We are the sum total of all the parts that go into the making of a life.

Because I thought the story of Dibs worth sharing, I have presented parts of this material to students in some of the lectures that I have given at universities and professional meetings.

One day I received a letter from a former student.

I couldn't help but take time out and write you this. I was only one of the hundreds in your class—and I probably wasn't even a face, but, believe me, I was an ear. I'm overseas now—in uniform again—and expecting to be moving up soon. In the barracks the other night I overheard a bit of conversation and all of America and home came rushing in. I remember you often said the important things are what we remember after we have forgotten everything else. And experiences can certainly force us to shift our focus. There we were the other night—discouraged, depressed, and wondering what in hell it was all about when all of a sudden Dibs was there. A fellow across the table was talking about Dibs. Can you imagine what that did to me? I wasted no time getting over to him. "How the hell did you hear about Dibs?" I asked him. He told me. It wasn't the same class; it wasn't the same year; it wasn't even at the same university. But it was the same kid all right. I don't need to tell you how much good it did me—not only me, but all of us—because together we told the rest of them the story. Dibs has become a symbol to us of all the values—the human values we try so hard to hold onto. And as the other fellow said, "With Dibs here, we can't lose."

But the thing that impressed me was how real Dibs was—what a real dynamic power he was—how he had become a part of me. And then I wondered about education. I got my degree in administration and I'm not too hip on a lot of psychological jargon and I'm sure I missed all the psychological implications of the case, but so help me God, Dibs is the only real person I ever met in a classroom who could teach me what it means to be a complete person—and to even go beyond that. I shall never forget those three lines: As I said I wanted it. As you said you wanted it. As we said we wanted it. I guess Dibs only wanted what we all want on a world-wide scale. A chance to feel worth while. A chance to be a person wanted, respected, accepted as a human being worthy of dignity.

Dib's family had moved to the suburbs and I had lost contact with him. Years passed. Then one day a friend of mine who was teaching in a school for gifted boys showed me a letter in the school's newspaper. It was addressed to the headmaster and faculty of the school. My friend did not know about Dibs. He did know that I was interested in any and all comments made by children that gave evidence of the understanding and courage they are capable of bringing to their daily life if they are given the opportunity to so state themselves. I read the open letter in the school newspaper:

This is an open letter of protest against the recent dismissal of one of my classmates and one of my friends. I am indeed indignant at your callousness and lack of understanding and feeling. It is whispered about that my friend was "suspended with dishonor" because he was caught cheating on examinations. My friend said he was not cheating and I believe my friend. He said he was verifying a date—an important date in history—and since accuracy of date is essential to establish its very existence, then it should indeed, be verified. I think you fail to understand the reasons why we sometimes do the things we do. Do you call it a fault when a person seeks to verify accuracy? Would you prefer that he cloud his honest doubt in ignorance? What are the purposes of examinations anyhow? Are they to increase our educational attainment? Or are they instruments used to bring suffering and humiliation and deep hurt to a person who is trying so hard to succeed?

One of the members of the teaching staff said to my friend in front of a group of us yesterday that if the pace of the school was too fast for him and he was forced to cheat to keep up, it would be better for him to go to another school. I am personally insulted by that remark. I am ashamed of my school if it does not maintain at all times an open door to any person who wants to come in and be with the rest of us. There are things far more important in this world than a show of authority and power, more important than revenge and punishment and hurt. As educators, you *must* unlock the door of ignorance ad prejudice and meanness. Unless my friend is given your apologies for this hurt he has received to his pride and self-respect and is reinstated, then I shall not return to this school this fall.

With sincerity and intent to act, I am,

Sincerely yours,
Dibs,

"How old is he now?" I asked.

"Fifteen."

"He writes an interesting letter," I commented. "What is he like?"

"He is a brilliant boy. Full of ideas. Concerned about everybody and everything. Very sensitive. A real leader. I thought you would enjoy this outraged outburst. And he acts on things he believes in. The school wouldn't want to lose him. They will probably follow his suggestion." He laughed. "Do you want to keep it for your collection of brave new words for justice and equality for all?"

"Thank you," I said. "With sincerity and intent to act." I believe that."

Author's Note

THE WEEK AFTER the play therapy sessions ended, a clinical psychologist administered a Stanford-Binet Intelligence Test to Dibs, who was very interested and cooperative. He established a good relationship with the examiner, whom he had never seen before. Results of this test gave an I.Q. of 168.

A reading test was also administered at this time. Dibs' reading score was years beyond his age and grade level. He was still answering all the questions correctly when he terminated the test by explaining to the examiner that he did not particularly care for this kind of reading that "jumped from one thing to another without reason." He told her that when he read he "preferred something that is ongoing and of real interest."

The test scores indicated that Dibs was an exceptionally gifted child who was using his intellectual capacities effectively.

Dibs' parents had given written permission for recording all therapy sessions, and for use of the recorded material, after appropriate disguise, for research, teaching, and publication, if the therapist felt that such a report would contribute to a better understanding of children. No therapy sessions are ever recorded by me without written permission from parents.

This book was written around those recorded sessions. The records have been edited to disguise all identifying information, to remove false starts, and some repetitious remarks, to facilitate a smoother report. The dialogue between Dibs and his therapist is essentially verbatum in sessions held in the Child Guidance Center. His mother's discussions are also drawn from the recordings of her sessions, but are not reported in full because some of the material was too personal and identifying, and did not specifically relate to Dibs.

However, no words were used that were not originally those of Dibs and his mother. A child, given the opportunity, has the gift of honest, forthright communication. A mother who is respected and accepted with dignity can also be sincerely expressive when she knows that she will not be criticized and blamed.

About the Author

VIRGINIA M. AXLINE was the author of *Play Therapy* and the acknowledged authority on the technique of play therapy in the treatment of emotionally disturbed children. Dr. Axline studied at Ohio State University and Columbia University. She taught for six years at New York University's School of Medicine and School of Education; for seven years she was on the faculty of Columbia University Teachers College and, prior to that, spent three years as a research associate and faculty member at the University of Chicago.